A Man Apart

By the same author

The First Fifty Years
The Night The Police Went On Strike
(*with G.W. Reynolds*)

A Man Apart

The British Policeman
and his Job

Anthony Judge

Arthur Barker Limited
5 Winsley Street London W1

ISBN 0 213   00459 X

Printed in Great Britain by
Redwood Press Limited
Trowbridge, Wiltshire

Contents

Introduction

The one hundred thousand men and women who belong to the British police service are members óf the most closely knit professional community in society. To be a policeman is to be part of an in-group which rejoices in its uniqueness. When the Royal Commission on the Police was given the task of deciding how much a constable ought to be paid, it found itself unable to fall back on the standard solution of comparisons with other occupations, because a policeman does a job which defies equation with any other. Policemen, in short, are different.

The story of how the New Police emerged under Peel and how the first metropolitan commissioners laid down for the force simple professional standards which have more or less been adhered to ever since, does not require tedious repetition here. The important thing to remember is that it was a deliberate act of policy to emphasize the wholly civilian nature of the police and make them independent of the political actions of government, subservient only to the law.

Parliament accepted the need for a professional police service only when it became obvious that the sòcial changes created by the Industrial Revolution meant that law enforcement and the maintenance of the Queen's Peace could no longer be left in the hands of volunteers or untrained local employees of doubtful worth. It was not that Parliament, or even Peel, suddenly had a great vision and thought what a splendid idea it would be to have a competent and trustworthy uniformed police force. Rather was it a case of accepting, with considerable reluctance, that what had appeared to be good enough for some hundreds of years would not survive the onrush of machines and the rapid growth of urban Britain. The police were a necessary evil, and as such they had to be carefully watched so that their powers did not make them the sort of oppressive police organization which flourished in Europe and revolted the politicians who made impassioned speeches about freedom in Westminster.

An undeniable achievement of the early police was that they overcame most of the hostility which greeted their appearance on the streets. They had to operate within a legal and judicial system which, for all its savage inhumanity towards offenders, was quite prepared to go to ridiculous lengths to uphold abstract concepts of liberty. In this way the murder of a policeman during a political riot could be described by a coroner's jury as justifiable homicide. Today the killing of a policeman shocks the public and brings a wave of sympathy for the police.

Throughout police history the dominant theme has been service to the community. The occasional crises which have occurred to impair the generally healthy relationship between the police and the public have involved issues of either integrity or the abuse of power. Ironically, the celebrations which marked the centenary of the Metropolitan Police in 1929 were marred by one trivial incident, the improper interrogation of a young woman involved in a morals case, which gave rise to a royal commission on police powers and procedure. Thirty years later, when an impudent youth had his ears boxed by two young constables in Thurso, all the cumbersome procedure of the Tribunals of Evidence (Inquiry) Act was invoked by the Prime Minister (after a full-scale debate in the House of Commons) to discover what had taken place. Shortly afterwards, an equally absurd incident between a traffic policeman and a civil servant led to the royal commission of 1960. What these incidents reflect is the deep-rooted belief of the British people that their police must be above reproach and that any example of policemen acting beyond their strictly prescribed powers must be dealt with. If, in pursuit of this ideal, Parliament sometimes over-reacts, the public feels that it is better to be ultra-cautious in the defence of liberty than to allow police bullies to think they can get away with anything. The public at such times takes a perverse delight in establishing its mastery over the police, although it is quite remarkable how consistently popular opinion will swing back to sympathy for them once it is felt that criticism has gone far enough. It is as if the public believes in keeping the police in their place, but accepts that the place which the police occupy in public esteem is secure.

It is something of a paradox that the one section of the community where there is real doubt about public esteem for the police is the force itself. Criticism of one of its members, or of police action on a specific occasion, is quickly regarded by policemen as an attack on the whole force. As Tony Smythe, secretary of the National Council for Civil Liberties (NCCL), told a Police Federation seminar in 1971, criticism outside the force of the police might be proportional to the lack of criticism from within. Smythe considers that police dislike for his tiny organization amounts at times to paranoia. For their part, the police regard NCCL as being in business for the specific purpose of making their lives difficult. In much the same way, one newspaper article attacking the police is sufficient for many policemen to classify the entire press as 'anti-police'.

'We're always reading articles where someone's complaining about the police,' said a London policeman, 'but how often do you read anything about all the times when we're helping people, saving lives, or just doing our job?' The simple explanation, that the press concentrates upon the bad policemen just because they are so rare and because what they do is so different from what the police are acknowledged to be, does not satisfy the police that they are getting fair treatment. In the recent past, the ability of minority groups to produce articulate spokesmen to condem police actions against their activities, and to mobilize publicity in support of their allegations, has given adverse statements on the police greater weight than used to be the case. Faced on occasion with a barrage of criticism, the police tend to make the mistake of taking the noise for the substance of public opinion. When Nixon discovered the modern phenomenon of society's 'silent majority', policemen might have noted that clamour and protest do not in themselves amount to a vote of censure on their service.

The police have been set apart from their fellow citizens in order to maintain liberty under the law by operating legal restraints against offenders. Put at its lowest, this means that the police do society's dirty work. They exist solely because law requires to be enforced, because someone has to be able to say that some forms of human behaviour are unacceptable and someone must have the authority to forbid them. 'The police can't expect to be loved,' said a chief constable, 'but they must be respected. The public will complain if a policeman is over-zealous and makes a bad mistake, but in time they will make allowances for human error. What the public won't forgive is police incompetence. If the idea ever got around that the police could no longer cope with crime, respect would go and we would be finished.'

Faced with the timeless dilemma of 'who police the police?' society has created elaborate safeguards against the danger of the police abusing their powers against the citizen. The laws of evidence and the British trial system are based upon both the assumed innocence of all accused persons until the contrary is proved and the repugnance felt against police methods which offend against a vague concept of fairness. Thus the Judges' Rules prohibit (or at least severely restrict) interrogation of prisoners, the police are obliged to warn suspects of their right to remain silent, juries must be kept ignorant of the criminal records of defendants, policemen must not offer inducements of mercy in order to produce confessions, and so on. There are controls on the power of the police to enter private property, particularly a man's home. In most parts of Britain the policeman does not have the power to stop and search a citizen on 'reasonable suspicion', a power which the police of London (and some other cities) do have, and find very convenient, although it is strongly resented by civil libertarians.

There cannot be an experienced policeman anywhere in Britain who doubts that some sacrifice of individual liberty would lead to a dramatic improvement in both the total number of crimes reported to the police and in the detection rate. Yet the police do not clamour for the law to be changed to make their jobs easier. They grumble about restrictions on their working methods and the facility of lawyers to exploit every loophole, but they still (at least in the vast majority of cases) work within the law and accept its limitations on their efficiency.

Understanding between the police and the public is not helped by the tendency of both sides to think in general terms. The public sees the police as one large uniformed body, made up of men who look alike, think alike, are alike, all cloaked in anonymity, doing a job which is necessary and admirable yet vaguely distasteful. The police see the public as people who do not belong to the force, people who cannot understand what a police force does and probably do not care so long as they are not affected. It is odd that a body which takes pride in its non-military status and tends to despise the armed forces as lower beings should describe all members of the public as 'civilians'.

It is possible to find within the ranks of a police force as wide and dissimilar a section of the community as would be found in, for example, a city suburb with a population ranging from wage-earners to the middle levels of management with a sprinkling of professional men. This is the sort of ward that generally elects Conservative councillors but will swing to Labour in a good year for the left, the district that sociologists would term a microcosm of the suburban community. Policemen may share common group attitudes, such as a belief in retributive justice and the deterrent value of capital punishment, because common professional experiences tend to create general conclusions. Yet to suggest that all policemen are alike in everything is nonsense. Some are dedicated, some are apathetic, a few are hostile to the job they are doing, just as in any commercial firm employees will be found who live for their work, many who regard it simply as a means of earning a living, and some who hate the organization and everything it stands for.

The danger of regarding all policemen as being the same is that public expectations of the police are based on false premises. Because the overall reputation of the British police stands high, it becomes natural to expect, even to take it for granted, that every policeman is dedicated to his job, competent at catching thieves, absolutely honest, courageous, dependable. The respectable citizen who almost never has to speak to a policeman tends to look at the police, in so far as he ever gives them a thought, in this light. The picture is not totally misleading as an impression of the whole body, but when such a citizen meets a policeman who falls short of expectations, who is rude or oppressive, stupid or uninterested, immediately the whole force is judged on one bad example.

Citizens who belong to minority groups are just as quick to generalize in terms of police failures. 'It seems to me,' said a radical student who serves on the committee of the National Union of Students, 'that the police attract a certain type of individual who has been brought up to accept authority without question, who enjoys being in a position to order other people around.'

'Most policemen are prejudiced against immigrants,' said an Indian who has worked for improved community relationships in Britain for twenty years. 'They accept the general attitudes of white people and listen to Enoch Powell.'

'It might be an idea if, before a geezer was aloud [sic] to be a copper, he was given a test just to make sure that he was a human being,' wrote Frank Norman, former criminal turned author.*

*The Police and the Public, (London, 1962)

Other minority or special-interest groups will have similar, though less enthusiastic points to make about the police. 'Coppers take a bloody delight in busting you,' said a youth convicted of possessing cannabis. 'They haven't a clue whether it's a bad thing or not.'

Because these are minority voices, belonging to people whose activities attract more hostility than sympathy from the general public, their criticisms of the police are dismissed as biased, distorted or plainly untrue. Yet when the chairman of the AA or the RAC accuses the police of conducting a war against motorists, thousands of victims of such persecution echo their 'hear hears'. And the man who complains in the train that 'the police are never there when they're wanted, too busy rushing around in Panda cars to be bothered with catching criminals' will get nods of agreement from middle-class commuters who feel uneasy about the safety of their homes. The lesson appears to be that the public at large will not be too disturbed if the police occasionally overstep the mark in enforcing laws that they approve of, just so long as they go easy on the ordinary citizen and concentrate on his protection.

But who and what are the police? The simple phrase 'the police' takes in the whole monolithic mass of men and women in blue, detectives and traffic police, cadets, horses and dogs (or at any rate their handlers), blue lamps and Pandas, suave murder specialists from Scotland Yard and pencil-licking half-literate bumpkins asking, 'What's all this 'ere?' It includes the chief constables, the court ushers, crime prevention and road-safety officers, fingerprinters and photographers, scenes-of-crime investigators, administration clerks, even the men who stand for hours outside royal residences or wander through the corridors of Westminster. They are all 'the police'. The station officer who takes details of lost property and the Special Branch officer keeping secret watch on subversion are in the same job, receiving (give or take an allowance or two) the same pay, subject to the same conditions of service and under the same discipline. Whatever the task performed, a member of the police service is a holder of the ancient office of constable, from whence comes the whole of his authority.

Anyone with elementary knowledge of the police organization could make a list of the manifold duties performed by members of the force and say that that is what the police do, but the reader would be no nearer to finding out what is more important: what the police are, and what kind of human beings live and work in the police community.

In succeeding chapters I have endeavoured to open doors for the citizen who might want an answer to such questions. Not that the doors have ever been closed. It is just that very few people seem sufficiently interested to learn what is on the other side.

Some explanation of the structure of the police, and a fairly general appraisal of the police as a body of workers, would not be out of place in this introduction. Some of the matters mentioned in the next few paragraphs will be repeated and enlarged upon later, but others, although important, will not fit neatly into chapters intended to increase the reader's understanding of the police as men and women.

To begin with, the British police service is not yet a national one. In England and Wales there are some forty-seven police forces, ranging from the Metropolitan Police with close on twenty thousand members to the smaller county forces with slightly below one thousand men. As recently as 1966 there were more than twice as many forces, but mergers have occurred as part of a rapid and far-reaching reorganization set in motion when Mr Roy Jenkins was briefly in charge of the Home Office.

The police, although they are a civilian body reposing great personal responsibility in the newest recruit (and in law this responsibility is virtually unchanged below chief constable status), have nevertheless a rigid caste system of higher ranks. This hierarchical structure separates policemen according to status. At the bottom of the promotion ladder are the great majority of the force (seven to eight out of ten), the constables. First move up is to sergeant, then to inspector. The Metropolitan Police has an intermediate rank of station sergeant which is expected to be abolished quite soon. Inspectors are often mistakenly referred to, even by the police, as 'officers', in the sense that the military speak of holders of the Queen's Commission. Inspectors are the lowest rank to wear uniform of different cut from that of the ordinary ranks, although here again it is probable that the service will eventually go over to a common uniform for all ranks, with status differences being marked by badges of rank. Inspectors and above, when mentioned by name, are called 'Mister'. They are entitled to be saluted by constables and sergeants and most forces require these observances in their standing orders. In some forces where discipline has been maintained at a higher level than usual, constables and sergeants stand up when an 'officer' enters the room.

Policemen can be any age between nineteen and fifty-five (or older in some cases). They must be at least five feet eight inches tall, physically fit and of average intelligence. They are paid between one thousand and just over four thousand pounds a year, according, of course, to rank and service, and enjoy certain fringe benefits such as a house or rent allowance big enough to repay a mortgage, and the prospect of being able to retire ten to fifteen years earlier than nearly every other wage-earner in the country.

The civilian police share another military characteristic in that their conditions of service are governed by regulations. These cover their pay and allowances, pensions, promotion, discipline, and a number of other matters connected with police organization. Unlike the military, police regulations are not decreed by some remote body. The police themselves have a considerable say. There exists a body called the Police Federation. It is supposed not to be a trade union, because once there was a police union, albeit an unofficial one, which twice tried to take the police out on strike and once succeeded. Indeed, it was doing so well for the downtrodden policeman of the First World War that it had to be suppressed by the Act of Parliament which installed the Police Federation as a sort of American company union or genteel staff association. For the first forty years of its existence, the Federation was nothing more than a safety valve for discontent and a none-too-reliable sounding board of police opinion. Changes during the 1950s allowed the Federation to have funds of its own and some of the restrictions on association with people outside the force were eased. Today the Federation is a highly effective representative and negotiating body, capable when the need arises of displaying as much militancy as is possible for a body whose members are denied the right to strike.*

The Federation represents authority's only concession to the modern concept of industrial democracy. Policemen, from the day that they take their oath of office, surrender their right to strike or take part in politics, and accept the various restrictions on their private affairs imposed by the Police Regulations. Furthermore, they become amenable to the Police Discipline Code, with all its sanctions against such minor offences as being late for duty or appearing untidy in uniform and the more heinous sins of bribery and corruption. It is implicit in the regulations that a constable gives his whole time to the service. Apart from his normal daily work lasting eight hours, he is expected to act as a policeman at all times. Because he is never 'off duty' he is unable to have a professional and a private existence, both neatly compartmented. Thus a policeman who associates with a married woman outside working hours is liable to be accused of discreditable conduct and punished accordingly. He would certainly be guilty of neglect of duty if he turned away from anything which required his attention as a policeman, although there are certainly occasions when he finds himself doing this, if his professional obligations conflict with his

*See also G.W. Reynolds and A. Judge, *The Night the Police Went on Strike* (London, 1968)

attempts to live as a private person.

Each of the forty-seven police forces is largely self-contained, with its own chief officer and local Police Authority of elected councillors and nominated magistrates. Ratepayers have to find approximately half the cost of running their police forces, but Police Authorities lack complete autonomy. In return for the Exchequer contribution, central government imposes rigid controls on police forces, mainly through the operation of common regulations and standards and the general oversight of the service vested in the Secretary of State.

The Home Office, through its Police Department, issues 'guidance' to chief constables which has the effect of instructions. In London there is no Police Authority of elected or nominated members as the force is the direct responsibility of the Home Secretary and ratepayers simply foot half the bill without any form of representation.

There is today an apparently irreversible trend towards greater centralization in police administration, with central government having more and more influence on policy and administration. A logical outcome of this development would be a single national police force. Only the same attitude of suspicion towards such a body as has been present throughout police history stands in the way of one unified force for England and Wales. The police themselves realize that increased urbanization and the greater mobility of the population have lessened the significance of force boundaries. This, in turn, has led to the establishment of such things as regional crime and traffic squads, regional recruit-training schemes, criminal record offices, radio networks and forensic science laboratories. The government's plans for local government reorganization will make further reductions in the number of police forces by 1974 and create huge urban forces for the new metropolitan authorities. The test of whether an administrative county will have its own force will be its viability as an efficient police unit. Further amalgamations can only weaken still further the already tenuous links with localities and hasten the day when a national police service becomes a reality.

This lessening in the sense of identity with a particular area has been most marked inside the service. In the not-too-distant days when every town of any size boasted its own police force, men joined a particular force and fully expected to remain there throughout their careers. In the counties, it was always understood that a policeman could be moved at a moment's notice to serve anywhere his chief constable directed. The borough policeman sacrificed his chances of rapid promotion and accepted greatly limited opportunities in return for the family security (including the right to live in his own home) which serving in one place brought to him. The direct human consequence of the sweeping amalgamations of the sixties was that this element of security was lost unless men were prepared to forego most of their promotion prospects by insisting on remaining in their former force areas. The county men, with no such inhibitions, lost little in promotion opportunities and gained a great deal, as chief constables, for the sake of uniformity, withdrew their objections to county policemen becoming home-owners and gave them the same facilities as former borough men.

A new generation of policemen is emerging. They are young men to whom local ties mean very little, who are at home with the new methodology and technology of the modern police service which is so totally different from the strictly traditional force that survived for so many years. The police today have many more young men who are able to think of their job in terms of its national significance, who will see in such national developments as the giant police computer network, due to be completed within the next few years, and the growing influence of the Home Office Research and Development Branch, a natural movement towards greater efficiency. Their older colleagues will be less enthusiastic and more suspicious of gimmickry, but the change in outlook of the whole service will become more noticeable as the seventies move on.

There is some risk that the police service, in the pursuit of greater efficiency through technology, will lose some of the ordinary humanity which has distinguished it over the years. Large police organizations are no more immune from depersonalization than huge automated factories. In such a situation, the attitude of working policemen as individuals becomes a question of major importance. With the current heavy emphasis on increased police efficiency as a means of combating crime, there is a tendency to judge a police force by its success in apprehending offenders. Sir Derek Capper chief constable of Birmingham, said in June 1971 at the Police Federation seminar, Kenilworth, 'The idea of the policeman which has emerged is that of the man catching criminals or wasting time in the enforcement of petty traffic law, when he should have something better to do. This idea has taken life. Even youngsters entering the service are sometimes conditioned by this concept. The practising policeman has immense public pressures thrust upon him.'

If this is truly the popular idea of what a policeman does, the image has been created by television fiction and the insistence of the police public relations officers in concentrating upon the criminal aspect. The pressures referred to by the chief constable of Birmingham are put upon the policeman by forces inside the service as well as outside. The chairman of a police authority looks for increased detection rates and a falling crime total to convince himself that the local force is doing its job. The public at large wants to hear of policemen making spectacular arrests of major criminals. There is much less concern to know that in a year's work the force's road-safety officers visited every local school to educate children in the dangers faced on the road, less still to know that, for example, the Metropolitan Police employs 150 middle-ranking policemen to work full time as community relations officers, seeking better relationships with immigrants.

It is because of the service rendered by the police to the community in so many fields that bear little or no relation to crime that they have won their way into public esteem. Essentially, it is a question of the respect that the ordinary citizen has for that solid, dependable, always helpful and astonishingly knowledgeable fellow citizen, the policeman. If the public were ever to feel that the price to be paid for a super-efficient police service making life impossible for the criminal was a loss of those other fairly indefinable qualities which make up the police, it might consider that price too high.

The commonest complaint about the police today is that they are nothing like as ubiquitous as they once were. The diminishing number of police officers walking the streets in uniform (an anomalous situation when there have never been so many police in the country) is generally deplored, and not least in rural areas where crime was never a major social problem. In this sense of public loss can be detected a feeling that the British policeman ought to be one of the few constant factors in a rapidly changing society.

If, as the experience of almost twenty years has convinced me, the ordinary citizen regards the policeman in a much better light than he himself appreciates, it must follow that he is prepared to take some interest in what a policeman's lot, in this hectic age, consists of. Hence this book.

I have quoted freely from many friends and colleagues all over the country. Names have been omitted because, firstly, they would mean little to those who do not know them and, secondly, they were not speaking for the specific purpose of being quoted for publication. And, as some of the views expressed are controversial, I have had to bear in mind the fact that there is such a thing as the Police Discipline Code and that, even if that sanction is not used, the police service suffers like any other large organization from a minority of petty and occasionally vindictive senior managers.

In attempting to convey to the reader something about the men who serve in the police, about the police as an organization and the interaction of their work and their daily lives, I have sought to convey my own deep respect and affection for the most unappreciated people in the force, the working constables who shoulder most of the work and receive least recognition.

Anthony Judge, 1971

1 Manpower

The rule of law in Britain is maintained by a police service of about one hundred thousand men and women. If this seems a large number, it should be related to the attendance at Wembley for the FA Cup Final. The police have a constant responsibility which requires them to operate every day of the year, twenty-four hours a day. In practice, this means that the maximum number of police on duty at any time of the day is never more than thirty thousand and in the 'off-peak' hours from midnight to early morning it may be no more than ten per cent of the total strength.

Each police force has what is called an 'authorized establishment'. This is the figure which has been approved by the Home Secretary as the optimum number of men and women who should be employed by the force. In England and Wales in October 1970, the total authorized establishment was one hundred and eight thousand and the actual number of police was ninety-two thousand. The obvious conclusion to be drawn is that the service needs another sixteen thousand police to reach its full strength, but this assumes that the authorized-establishment figures are realistic. There are two views about establishments. One is that they underestimate the real needs of the police, the other is that they are grossly inflated and unscientific.

The latter view was expressed by *The Economist* (5 December 1970):

'The claim that there is a serious shortage of police manpower is specious . . . How precisely are establishments calculated, and on what basis?

The answer, in practice, is the local chief constable.

Certainly, he has to discuss the matter with his local Home Office inspector of constabulary, and get his agreement, and obtain the support of his police authority. But there is little evidence that inspectors of constabulary apply a critical yardstick to demands for higher establishments, and still less that police authorities are prepared to challenge the professional judgment of their chief constables.'

Establishments in each force are, in truth, very much a matter of the chief constable's personal evaluation of its needs. Until a few years ago, chief constables' salaries were related to the establishments, and it was thought that this encouraged them to apply for increases in the figures, but the suggestion that the current establishment figures are artificially high finds few supporters inside the service.

It is true that the total establishment figure has swollen surprisingly throughout the 1960s. The decade opened with an authorized establishment for England and Wales of seventy-six thousand and an actual strength of seventy thousand. In just over ten years, therefore, the actual number of police has increased by over twenty-two thousand, but the establishment figure has gone up by thirty-two thousand. Obviously, if the theoretical number of police required continues to outstrip the actual strength in this way, the 'shortage' of police will appear to be getting worse, no matter how many extra men and women are recruited.

The explanation for the huge rise in establishments is that, from the outbreak of the war in 1939 until the early sixties, they were virtually frozen by the Home Office, which saw no point in approving increases until the existing figures had been reached. Not only did this render the establishments meaningless, it was also a convenient and effective way of hiding from public view the true shortage of police. When the Home Office, following criticism from the Royal Commission on the Police 1960-2, was obliged to change its policy and permit forces to review their theoretical needs, some chief constables, aided and abetted by Home Office inspectors (who are all former senior policemen), may have allowed their enthusiasm to run away with their judgement. However, the figures now appear to have reached something approaching their maximum.

The Research and Development Branch of the Home Office's Police Department has been investigating the problem of how to determine a realistic establishment for a police force for at least five years and may yet be years away from an acceptable solution. The Branch, a group of senior policemen and scientists who work together on various police problems that might be amenable to scientific assistance, has been examining the police role in terms of the functions performed by the various departments of the force.

Many policemen would be sceptical about the chances of the Research and Development Branch emerging with a practical formula for measuring the policing requirements of the country in terms of manpower.

'A scientist might think he can say that it takes x number of police to control a town of, say, a hundred thousand people,' a chief constable said to me, 'but local factors make a nonsense of that. I would want to know more about how the population was made up, what its traffic problems were, how many crimes were committed last year, and all kinds of purely local considerations.'

Whatever the argument about its precise size, that there is still a serious shortage of police in Britain's industrial areas is undeniable. One man who is convinced of this is M. Jean Nepote, the Director General of the International Police Organization (Interpol), who considers that the police strength of Great Britain would be more appropriate to a mainly rural country, than to one of the most densely populated and industrialized nations of the world.

While preparing this book, I was struck by the apparent lack of awareness among many policemen that the actual strength of the service had grown so rapidly in such a short time. Often, when I quoted the gain of twenty thousand in ten years, the immediate reply was something like, 'Where the hell are they, then?' and there is a common feeling in the service that there are fewer policemen doing the actual police work today than there were a few years ago.

This has been said to me often enough by policemen of the rank of inspector and above, those who have the task of finding enough men to meet the day-to-day requirements of the force, especially for street duty. These men sincerely believe that they are no better off for manpower now than they were ten years ago. Their bewilderment is all the more understandable when it is appreciated that, side by side with the growth of the service, there has been a vast increase in the numbers of non-police personnel employed by every force (the people described by all policemen as 'civilians' to denote their status as outsiders). There was just a handful of traffic wardens in 1960. By 1970 there were almost five thousand and the numbers were increasing. Civilians employed in various capacities by police forces numbered twenty-three thousand in full-time jobs and over five thousand part-timers. In 1960 there were fewer than eight thousand civilian employees.

Although more and more duties that do not require a trained police officer are now carried out by civilians, such as clerical work and manning the telephone switchboards, it is doubtful whether the objective of civilianization, releasing policemen to do police work, has been achieved as completely as was intended. Policemen do not exactly welcome civilian assistance with open arms. Some insist that it is wrong that confidential police matters should be handled by non-police personnel. Others believe that replacing policemen with civilians leads to less efficiency, not more. 'Our chief constable admits that he needs two civvies to do the same job that one policeman used to do,' said a West Country constable. 'When we were in the court office, a policeman would do all his own records and filing and type the summonses. Now you find that a typist does the typing and a clerk does the filing. They don't have the same interest that we had, and they are strictly nine-to-five in outlook.'

There is, however, a more deep-rooted reason for the passive animosity which the policeman displays towards the encroachment of outsiders into what was once an exclusively police situation—the police station. It is due, in part, to a feeling that it is dangerous to admit civilians to knowledge of matters that should be confidential to policemen. There is also a belief that the employment of civilians has cut down the opportunities for older policemen to find some niche away from the full rigours of outside duty. I have heard the same policeman who is scornful of the competence and practical experience of chairbound colleagues argue in almost the same breath that they should not be replaced by someone from outside the force. Something of both attitudes was evident in the debates at the Police Federation conference in 1969, when resolutions condemning the influx of civilians into police affairs were carried by overwhelming majorities. The policeman feels that in some way his professional pride is affronted if others begin to do the work that he has always done. In this he is no different from other groups of workers, but whereas the docker or the printer is cocooned by union restrictions on the use of outside labour, the policeman has no say in the decision taken by management to civilianize a police department.

Suspicion and resentment have also been a police reaction to the introduction and increase of traffic wardens. In essence, the warden has relieved the town policeman of one of his most onerous and thankless tasks. During the fifties, when the parking problem became really serious, town police forces had to use most of their available daytime strengths to keep the streets clear. Young policemen who had joined the service to fight crime hated this work, which had a disastrous effect on relations between the policeman and the motorist. The warden has inherited both the job and the hostility that goes with it. Yet many policemen see in the traffic warden a threat to their own status. They regard him as the forerunner of the fully fledged traffic policeman. This is why even the small extension of the duties of wardens, such as allowing them to direct moving traffic and report vehicle licence offences, has been received with suspicion. When, a few years ago, the Metropolitan Police attempted to improve the status and quality of the wardens by introducing a simple rank structure, policemen felt that their worst fears for the future were being confirmed. In any discussion with policemen on pay, they will refer to the fact that the basic pay of a traffic warden in London is close to the starting rate of a constable (although the latter's allowances and overtime earnings give him a substantial lead).

The trend towards employing more civilians on 'non-police' duties was accelerated by a report published in 1967 by a working party on manpower which was set up by the Police Advisory Board, the body which comprises representatives of the police and the authorities and advises the Home Secretary on police matters. This said that police should ordinarily undertake only those duties which require a combination of the 'special qualifications and personal qualities demanded on entry to the service' (whatever they might be), the particular training provided within the police, and the exercise of police powers. One field suggested by the working party as ripe for civilian assistance was the section of the force which works on the scenes of crimes, fingerprinting and photography. The scenes-of-crimes officer attends the location of an offence to search for such evidence as fingerprints or things which might be useful to forensic science laboratories, such as clothing fibres. The introduction of civilian scenes-of-crimes officers in the Metropolitan Police met with strong protests from the police in the CID. They had two objections, the first being that the recruitment of civilians closed an avenue of specialization for the policeman, and the second that this could be a 'back door' method of securing a system of direct entry to the CID. It was noted that civilian applicants for these jobs were required to have educational qualifications which were much higher than anything expected of a policeman.

The policeman's general feeling that a civilian employee is

an unwarranted intrusion into the police community is sometimes reflected in his personal relationships with non-police personnel. 'If you ring up any criminal record office,' said one detective, 'you can tell without asking whether you are talking to a policeman or a civilian. If it's a retired policeman doing a civvy job, it's not so bad, but if it's just a records clerk you don't get the same service. They don't know what we want because they don't know the language. A copper in records knows what you're after, and he often gives you a good idea of who you are looking for, just from the description of the job and odd scraps of information.'

It must have been something of a shock for some senior officers to discover the difference between giving orders to policemen and to civilians who were supported by trade unions. When the strike of the council workers in 1970 looked like spreading to all manual grades, at least one chief constable found that key workers in his force headquarters would have to be replaced by policemen to keep operating, a situation which would have brought the force perilously close to accusations of strike breaking.

The views the police may hold about the drawbacks of civilian assistance are positively mild compared with the intense dislike which most policemen have for the Special Constabulary. 'They are bloody blacklegs,' said a forthright Manchester constable. 'Can you think of any other job in Britain which would let a bloke come in and do another worker's job for nothing?'

The inspectors of constabulary and chief constables go to great lengths to encourage the development of the Special Constabulary but they know quite well that there is a very limited use for an unpaid auxiliary police force and they are aware of the hostility of the regulars. Public-spirited citizens are encouraged to join the Specials in the belief that they will be giving the hard-pressed policeman much needed aid. Often they are surprised, disappointed and eventually discouraged by the indifference and antipathy of the regulars.

The police attitude is conditioned by the natural trade-union approach of any worker who sees another man doing his job for nothing, and a sense of professional pride. 'It took me ten years to learn this job, and I'm still learning,' said a London sergeant. 'Are you going to tell me that three nights in a classroom and once round the beat in a car makes a civvy into a policeman?.'

The Home Office working party mentioned previously, while encouraging the recruitment of more Specials, was careful to take account of police feelings. It recommended that Specials should not perform more than an average of four hours' duty a week and that this should take the form of training of the kind that a Special would need if he were mobilized in an emergency.

A Kent officer thought that the Special Constabulary was unlikely to be of real assistance to the police, but thought that most regulars made too much unnecessary fuss about them. 'We have a good crowd of Specials in this area,' he said, 'most of them are City types, commuters, and they think the world of the police. They don't take our jobs and they don't affect our overtime. I think it's a good thing that there are nice solid people like these willing to help us.' His is a view unlikely to be shared by the lower ranks of the police, although most regulars would acknowledge that most Specials are well-intentioned. Many county forces have relied on Specials to assist them with seasonal problems such as weekend traffic control, but an expansion of the size and scope of the Special Constabulary would appear to be both unlikely and highly unpopular with the regular police.

In a later chapter I shall be discussing the problems of recruitment and wastage in the police, which are inseparable from any consideration of manpower. Whatever the future holds for the police, either by way of a welcome and unexpected influx of additional men or of a worsening of the present serious position, the proper and effective use of a policeman has become more important than ever before.

It is only in the last five years or so that the police have given really serious attention to this question. Before then, a reincarnated Rowan (one of the first Metropolitan Commissioners of Police) would have found little significant change in the policing methods of the twentieth century compared with those he and his colleague Richard Mayne introduced for the New Police a few years after Waterloo. 'Without denigrating him as a human being, we have to look upon a policeman in much the same light as a manufacturer would regard a very valuable piece of equipment,' said a chief constable. 'If he is not properly used for the job he was intended for, then he is wasted.'

Chief constables have the problem of reconciling their manpower shortage with their increasing commitments. Mr Walter Stansfield produced an illuminating booklet in 1970 which explained some of his problems as chief constable of Derbyshire. Looking back over the previous twenty years, he reported that the number of police in the county had grown in that period from 816 to 1,142, an increase of just over forty per cent. Thanks to the reduction of the policeman's working week from six days to five, however, the actual increase in available manpower was just over twelve per cent. This helps to explain what a Yorkshire inspector mentioned as 'the mystery of the disappearing policemen'. Meanwhile, the work expected of an individual constable in Derbyshire has risen dramatically. Nearly twenty-two thousand crimes were reported in the county in 1969, four times as many as the 1949 figure. There has also been a four-fold increase in the number of locally registered motor vehicles and an increase of more than one half in the number of accidents involving personal injury. At the same time as Mr Stansfield was publicizing his problems, local traders in Derby were planning to employ private security patrols to look after their shops at night, because the chief constable had told them that he could not deploy policemen for this task.

Mr Stansfield believes that there ought to be 1,800 policemen in Derbyshire, an increase of 300 on his authorized establishment and 650 on his present strength. He knows that nothing short of a miracle would be required to obtain such a boost to his resources. All chief constables have found that the increase in actual strengths over the past two decades has been totally inadequate to keep pace with rises in population and the pressures of crime and traffic upon the force. These are the factors which have compelled the service to shake off its traditional conservatism and revolutionize its organization.

The major change of recent years, and the one which may have the most far-reaching consequences for the future, was not the result of a police initiative at all. In 1966 the then Home Secretary, Roy Jenkins, announced a totally unexpected and sweeping reorganization of the individual police forces. The plan was to reduce the patchwork of 125 separate police forces to just under fifty. The borough forces were swallowed by the surrounding county forces, except for the largest cities such as Liverpool, Birmingham, Manchester, Bristol, Sheffield and Leeds (later joined after much local lobbying by Bradford and Hull). In addition, there were mergers of adjoining counties. With few exceptions, all the new forces were to have at least a thousand men and some, like Lancashire with close on seven thousand and West Yorkshire with over four thousand, became very large forces by former standards.

Jenkins pleaded enhanced efficiency as justification for his actions and he was supported by most expert opinion, including the Police Federation. The scheme did not require legislation as it was possible to merge forces under the Police Act 1964. Thus Jenkins was able to overcome the vocal and usually powerful opposition of the local authorities, who resented losing their individual forces and complained bitterly at the complete absence of consultation. Looking back, it is remarkable to see just what Jenkins had achieved. With one stroke, he had done what his Home Office advisers were convinced it would take at least twenty years to accomplish, under the leisurely arrangements which had existed before 1966 for merging small forces. Suddenly, forces of the size of those of Nottingham and Leicester among the cities, and of many sizeable counties, where amalgamation had never been contemplated, found a date set for their extinction as separate units. The Police Authorities which resisted the schemes, and spent the ratepayer's money on legal fees for public inquiries, found that the reports of these tribunals simply rubber-stamped the overall strategy of the plan. Much to everyone's surprise, the amalgamations were complete before the Labour Government went out of office.

It was said that an important associated benefit of having fewer and larger police forces would be greater opportunities for career-minded policeman. This is undoubtedly true, but so is the fact that the amalgamations had the opposite effect on many policemen who were serving in the smaller forces and suddenly found themselves part of a much larger organization. Whatever case might be made out for such changes on grounds of operational efficiency, the effect on policemen, both as individuals and as members of forces, was one of the least considered factors in the Jenkins plan.

The members of the smaller forces found themselves in much the same position as the employees of any small firm that is about to be taken over by a large competitor.

'I joined the borough so that I would be able to stay in one place all my service,' a Lancashire sergeant said, 'I knew that promotion chances were probably better in the county, but I made a choice. We've known for years that there might be a change one day, but that hasn't made it any easier now it's happened.'

It is the policeman who was quite contented to remain in one place and liked belonging to a small and fairly intimate unit who most feels that the recent changes have blighted his future. If previous experience of force amalgamations is anything to go by, it will be many years before the latent resentment of policemen who feel like this disappears. Amalgamations have undoubtedly weakened the strong local links which used to exist between the small borough forces and the communities they served. It may be that this loss cannot be replaced by any sense of ownership in the new larger, highly mechanized and seemingly ultra-efficient forces which have taken their place.

'We are moving closer and closer to a national police force,' a chief constable told me. 'The next step will be large regional police forces covering whole areas of the country, all linked in Whitehall under a central police authority.' Clearly, the existence of so many different police forces in England and Wales, in itself a legacy from the indiscriminate growth of the police service during the nineteenth century, was not fitted to the needs of today. Changes were inevitable, but the question which can only be answered by much longer experience of the 1966 reorganization (completed in 1969) is whether the police service is now more efficient and whether any positive contribution has been made to the correct use of police manpower. The amalgamations were not the only revolutionary change to affect the police service in the sixties. Science has come to the aid of the force in the shape of the personal radio. When some forces, such as those of Nottingham and Lancashire, began experimenting with primitive 'walkie-talkie' apparatus in the fifties, the rest of the service laughed. Yet today the radios play such a vital role in police operations that it is hard to realize what a recent innovation they are. They act as a constant link between the patrolling policeman and his base, the station. 'Knowing how hard these lads work now,' said a station sergeant in the Metropolitan, 'it seems hard to believe that just a few years back there was no such thing as a radio. The beat men just went out of the station and that was that. If anything happened and they couldn't get to a phone, it was just too bad. Now they just call in or we call them and give them a job to see to.'

There has also been a huge increase in the number of cars used by the police. Much against their own inclinations, for the belief in the effectiveness of the foot constable still persists, chief officers have been forced to put more and more men in cars. To the public, there is still something wrong with the sight of a policeman driving past in a car, but the motorized policeman has at least the advantage of mobility, and the ability to cover a much larger area.

The tenacity with which many policemen and most of the general public clings to the belief that the uniformed constable patrolling a beat on foot is the acme of police efficiency has remained unshaken throughout the rapid transformation of recent years. When Rowan and Mayne set out the working arrangements for the new Metropolitan Police, the beat system they laid down was simply an extension of the watch system which had existed for centuries. In reality, the beat man on his patrol was, for over a century and a quarter, little more use than a watchman, particularly at night. Alone and unarmed, the night constable had no means of summoning help except by blowing his whistle, and by the time it came, the offenders had as often as not disappeared. Since his work at night consisted mainly of checking shop doors, any thief with an ounce of organizational ability discounted the beat man as a serious threat to his plans.

It was the vast expansion of towns during the forties and fifties which caused the police, for the first time, to start to question their own methods, and especially that sacred cow, the man on the beat. In terms of the efficient use of manpower, and trained and intelligent manpower at that, the beat man working in the traditional way made little sense. The 'cover' he provided was purely theoretical. At any one time, his supervision of a beat depended on the extent of his vision and his physical presence. When, after the war, beats were stretched and often combined to make one man try to cover the ground of two and even three, the situation became farcical.

The personal radios alone would not have made much impact. They would only have provided a means of immediate communication, in itself a welcome development but, having got his message, the beat man would still have had to go on foot to the location of an incident. It is here that the mechanization of beats has made its mark. The public may miss passing the time of day with the patrolling policeman, but the man in the car is providing them with much better service.

But it is in the use of individual constables that the police service has made its most radical change. This is the era of the 'unit beat' system, far and away the most significant development in police organization. 'Unit beat policing' (UBP) owes something to the inspiration of Orlando Wilson, the legendary chief of the Chicago police, who first developed the idea of a greater link between the police patrolman and his neighbourhood. His ideas came to the notice of Sir Eric St Johnston, a former Chief Inspector of Constabulary, during his time as chief constable of Lancashire. St Johnston's interest in Wilson's work led to the first experiments in unit beat policing, a co-operative effort between the Lancashire force and the Research and Development Branch. This was in 1966.

Unit beat policing aimed to achieve five main objectives: increased police efficiency; a better understanding between police and public, through closer contact between the men on the beat and the residents and by swifter response to calls for assistance and complaints; better police information; the more economical use of manpower; and to give the police themselves, especially the young constable, a new challenge by heightening their interest in the job and making police work more interesting and full of incident.

Accrington, a town of some sixty thousand inhabitants, was chosen for the Lancashire pilot scheme. Before unit beat policing, there had been twelve individual beats for constables to patrol on foot, but with only forty-five constables in the division, it was quite impossible to provide a twenty-four-hour cover of each beat by one constable. The usual practice was to double up the beats, which meant that police effectiveness was strictly related to the shortage of men. Apart from the mainly industrial and commercial town centre, Accrington was divided, under the unit beat system, into eight distinct areas. Each area was further divided into two beats with a constable attached permanently to one beat. Ideally the unit beat man should live on his beat but this is not practicable for many reasons, such as the existing location of police houses or the undesirable nature of some district.

Each area of two adjoining beats was allocated a police car, the now familar Panda, and the idea was that the Panda should provide a twenty-four-hour cover whilst the beat constables worked their customary eight hours a day, choosing their own working times. In addition, each area was allocated a detective constable to deal with criminal investigation, working in close association with the beat men.

'I thought that unit beat working would collapse on this business of letting the men choose their own working times,' said a chief inspector, 'it seemed a bit like heresy. We've always been so disciplined and regimented about these things. I thought that if the lads were allowed to please themselves, they'd all choose nine to five, but I was wrong. By and large, they've played the game. They know the times that they're most needed and I suppose that we've got much better night cover than we used to have when they moaned like hell if they had to do an extra late turn or night.'

Conventional policing had required five men to cover each beat all the time, three men working eight hours each, with cover for days off, sickness and other contingencies. Under unit beat policing conditions, it was estimated that each two-beat area needed five uniformed men (including three to man the car) and a detective. The system was never intended to lead to a reduction in the overall strength of the police but it was meant to lead to a reduction in the rate of growth of the service.

This was the framework of the system, but it was far more than a simple and fairly obvious reconstruction of working methods. The resident constable, living and working all the time on one beat, was to be an important part of his community in a way that the beat constable, who might only appear in one district once a week for a few hours, could never be. The resident men were instructed to be the eyes and ears of the service. They were expected to get to know as many local residents as they could, especially the people they ought to know, the criminals. They were told to report everything, no matter how trivial it seemed to them, about known offenders and people suspected of shady activities. Merely to see a doubtful character walking in the street was worth noting because it established his whereabouts at a specific time, either eliminating him from suspicion of a particular crime or ruining his alibi by pinpointing his position. It was useful to know, also, that a man was spending money in a pub or bookmaker's, more so if he was known to be unemployed. 'It's what we call criminal intelligence,' said a senior officer of the Research and Development Branch, 'if you like, spying. Under the old system, one policeman might see a criminal and think no more about it, or he might know that another had a bit of money to spend who was flat broke the day before. Because nothing had happened on his beat he would do nothing about it. Now, we ask him to note and report everything. He never knows whether the most trivial and useless scrap of gossip about a man might just be the piece of the jigsaw we have been looking for.' All this miscellaneous information is collected at the divisional headquarters by a policeman known as 'the collator'. It is his job to gather all the items, and to disseminate those which might be of interest to others.

The unit beat scheme was commended by the 1967 report of the Police Advisory Board's working party on manpower. Within a very short time, thanks to the enthusiasm and sometimes forceful persuasion of reluctant chief constables by the inspectors of constabulary, it spread through the service. By 1970, unit beat policing was on the point of ousting conventional policing systems in the towns and was gaining a foothold in London.

In its attempt to bring the beat policeman closer to the small section of the community he serves, unit beat policing is akin to the traditional system of the village bobby, a man who has always enjoyed such a relationship with the public. Ironically, recent years have seen his numbers dwindling as more and more village constables have been withdrawn. In some county areas, unit beat policing or other experiments with rural policing systems have been introduced but, whereas in the towns these have given both the constables and the neighbourhoods they serve a sense of identity with each other, in the country this has been only a substitute for the village constable. The beat covered by the unit man in the country tends to be larger than his former village jurisdiction.

The ultimate success or failure of unit beat policing is going to depend on the calibre and enthusiasm of the men who are working the system. Some chief constables were dubious about it and resented the way in which they were pressured into adopting it to please the Home Office. In these forces, it is common to find local variations of the scheme, most of which cannot be described as improvements.

'How can I be a resident policeman,' said a Cornish policeman, 'when I'm called in to the station to do office duty every time the regular man is sick, or posted to the nearest coast traffic black spot in the summer to do point duty?' Another unit beat man complained to me that the area car was constantly engaged on ordinary divisional duties and rarely available when it was most needed.

'If we had enough men to work it,' said a superintendent, 'unit beat would be most of the answer to our problems, but not the complete one. It will never be that because it cannot take account of the different work put into it by different people.' This superintendent's division went over to unit beat policing in 1968. He had to allocate his available beat strength to the various beats. 'You'll always get the constable who can't be trusted to work without supervision. He's either the dull man who needs help from his sergeant and inspector, or he's the fly boy who'll do nothing at all unless someone's on his tail.'

As for the 'new challenge' aimed for in unit beat policing, the hopes appear to have been justified. It is not only the very young policeman who has responded to the impetus of greater responsibility and more job interest. 'UBP is full of faults, but it's a hundred per cent better than the way we used to work,' said a Lancashire constable with nearly twenty years' service. 'I thought I would get sick of working the same beat. When I first moved here, I moaned because it was the beat that everyone tried to keep off — lots of lock-up property to try at nights and as boring as hell. Now I wouldn't want to move. It's a different job now.'

Unit beat policing might prove to be one answer to one part of the police manpower problem — the more effective use of available strength — but it is the idea behind it, that of the resident constable living on his beat and being an active part of the community, that could be of greatest significance. 'I like my home beat men to get to know the kids in the schools,' said a unit inspector in London, 'and some of them have made good contacts which would never have been possible under the old beat system. Not every man is capable of doing this, you can't expect every policeman to be good at public relations, but the ones that have been able to reach the kids in this way seem able to keep on top of juvenile crime.'

A statistical answer to the problem of the 'disappearing policemen' at a time when there have never been so many men in the service is hard to find. Throughout the service, however, one finds complaints of 'top-heavy' administration departments, and an outsider paying a casual visit to any police headquarters would be struck by the abundance of uniformed officers working there. In a sense this may be part of the price to be paid for the greater sophistication of the service. Administration plays an ever-increasing role in force organization. Every headquarters has its various departments, each related to a particular activity of the force. Information rooms require mainly police staffs to control operations, there are departments for crime prevention, road safety, records, welfare, training, personnel and so on. Each specialist branch of the force, such as CID and traffic, requires its own administrative section. The extent to which these offices have been civilianized so that their police staffs are limited to duties which only police officers can perform varies from force to force, according to the chief constable's personal commitment to this policy.

It is easy to be critical of general manpower policies in the police service, but so much of the apparent waste of trained men on unnecessary tasks springs from the demands which outside influences put upon the police, not from their own stubborn determination to employ police on office duties. The Home Office requires the continual preparation of detailed statistics on every conceivable matter. Insurance companies require copies of police reports in every case where one of their customers says that a policeman attended an accident. The courts require voluminous information about persons charged. It all adds up to extra work for the police and the need for extra administrative staff.

One of the problems facing the Research and Development Branch in its quest for an exact formula for determining police establishments is the number of imponderables involved in police administration. It is one thing to say that there should be a given number of officers employed on beat, detective and traffic duties, but no one can forecast with any certainty how many of them will actually be available for duty at a given date. Time spent in court or in the preparation of a prosecution is one factor governing availability. It is estimated that the most simple offences can require a minimum of three hours' time devoted to paperwork and giving evidence. A criminal charge involving an arrest, remands at the magistrate's court, committal proceedings, trial and possible appeal, could run into hundreds of man-hours lost to the force.

The introduction of the Magistrates' Courts Act in the fifties gave offending motorists their first opportunity to have their 'crimes' dealt with by post, with a consequent saving in police time. Had it not been for this Act, there is no doubt that the work of the magistrates' courts would have ground to a complete standstill years ago, with a certain collapse of the administration of road traffic law. As it is, mounting pressures of all kinds have led to the fixed penalty system being introduced and extended. It is true that this, in its turn, has created a major problem for court staffs in the volume of unpaid penalties, but a similar delay at the beginning of the process would have meant complete chaos. We are unlikely to reach a stage where proceedings in the criminal courts can be simplified to the same extent. Paradoxically, a sudden rise in the amount of crime detected by the police would quickly result in two disasters – a mammoth bottleneck in the courts, where longer and longer delays in dealing with offenders have been the pattern of recent years, and a huge problem for the police as a greater number of police officers became caught up in the legal process.

The police service has lived with its manpower problem for a quarter of a century and no early solution is yet in sight. Meanwhile, the work load grows and intelligent observers, inside the service and out, begin to question the general ability of the police to cope with the anticipated problems of the seventies and eighties. A decade ago, the number of indictable crimes in Britain was just over half a million a year and there was a great deal of concern about general lawlessness. Today, we have more than a million such crimes being committed each year and the total rises annually. It would be comforting to say that the police service has coped surprisingly well up to now, and there is no reason why it should not continue to do so. Whether such an optimistic outlook is justified depends very much upon how well the service fares in recruiting extra manpower in the near future and, just as important, how effectively all available officers are to be used.

2 Recruiting

In terms of numbers, the police do not have a recruiting problem. They can rely upon getting between five and six thousand recruits a year. The manpower shortage is caused by three factors: the rapid growth of establishments, the early retiring ages of policemen, and the high rate of resignation, especially among young officers. Taken together, these reasons explain why the service has, since 1945, needed to recruit six men to be sure of a net gain of one.

The quality of recruits is another matter. For the past twenty-five years the service has been forced to compete for labour, a situation that would have been unthinkable in its previous history. Between the wars, the police constable was the aristocrat of working men. He had a wage that was at least as good as, and often better than, anything paid in industry. He had security, and the certainty of a good pension in his late forties or early fifties. Police forces did not have to advertise for recruits; there were at least ten applicants for every vacancy. The *Police Review* used to run a 'Candidate's Column', giving hints on how to gain extra weight or improve one's education, together with notes of forces that might have room for one or two men. Preference was given to men who had completed regular engagements in the army, especially the Brigade of Guards, and married men had little chance. Height standards of at least six feet, with corresponding weight and chest measurements, were common. The general rule was that local men were not appointed to forces near their homes. Even when it was decided, during the economic crises of the early thirties, that police pay was over-generous and a cut of ten per cent was made for new entrants, there were still more than enough recruits.

It was the war and its aftermath which produced a complete reversal of the recruiting situation. Thousands of policemen were recalled to the colours during the war and others were allowed to resign to join the forces. Their places were filled by wartime auxiliaries because it was confidently anticipated that they would return to the police. In fact, many of them decided on demobilization that they would be better off in industry, where wage rates had outstripped police pay. It was the reluctance of the authorities to make genuine improvements in pay and conditions in the immediate post-war period which created a manpower problem that has never been solved since.

The first real crisis came in 1949. Police strengths had fallen to around fifty thousand, since the men who had been retained in the service beyond pension age were allowed to go, and just under half of all the recruits appointed were leaving within a few months of joining. What was termed the 'crime wave' was providing a major problem and there were, for the first time, real doubts as to the ability of the police to cope. A Committee of Inquiry was appointed to examine police conditions and pay, with Lord Justice Oaksey as chairman. Unfortunately, the committee's report coincided with the Stafford Cripps wage freeze and devaluation, so that the modest pay increase which followed did little to improve the manpower position.

Throughout the fifties the story of neglect continued and it was not until the Royal Commission on the Police published an interim report on police pay in 1960 that any dramatic improvement occurred. The Commission awarded average increases of thirty per cent, bringing the experienced police constable into the then affluent thousand-a-year class. The Royal Commission virtually restored the policeman to his pre-war status. During the sixties, however, police pay negotiations were caught up in government efforts to impose an incomes policy so that by the end of the decade the service was just as dissatisfied with its pay as it had been before the Commission. All the same, there was during this period the most rapid expansion in numbers and at the end of the decade the service had reached the one hundred thousand mark for the first time.

One of the notable successes of the Police Federation was to persuade the authorities, in 1962, that future movements in police pay should be aimed at maintaining the standards set by the Royal Commission. The Police Council, which is the negotiating body on pay and conditions for all the police in the United Kingdom, agreed to review pay at intervals of two years, taking account of wage movements throughout the country. Subsequent negotiations have allowed police pay to keep pace with average wage movements, but have fallen down on Willink's assessment because the scope of the reviews has been too restricted. Willink looked at pay in a selection of occupations and added factors to take account of the unique responsibilities and arduous working conditions of the police. This 'formula' fitted the pay standards recommended in the Royal Commission's report (some people think that the Commission decided first on the amount that a constable should be paid, then looked around for a 'formula'). The Police Council, by looking only at the movements in national wage rates and ignoring the substantial improvements in industrial earnings, which include overtime and productivity bonus payments, has set an artificially low ceiling on police pay. Moreover, policemen know that the Willink 'formula' would today produce more than the current levels of pay.

In the spring of 1971 the Police Council concluded its 1970 pay review and the police received a pay increase which averaged about sixteen per cent. The Federations (in pay negotiations the Scottish Federation works with England and Wales, and Northern Ireland) had demanded a massive thirty-five per cent, based on their calculation of what the Willink formula would produce, plus an addition to take account of the large increase in the work burden carried by the police since 1960. The settlement represented an attempt by the authorities to stimulate pay because of the serious manpower situation.

As it happened, police manpower did improve in 1971. It would have been surprising, in a year when unemployment neared the million mark for the first time since before the war, if it had not done so. The improvement of close on three thousand in total police strengths was brought about by less resignations, few men becoming eligible to retire during the year, as well as more recruiting.

Police experience has been that the authorities are unreceptive to demands for improved pay and conditions when recruiting is fairly healthy. It was, therefore, a pleasant surprise for the police when, just prior to Christmas 1971, the Federations asked for, and promptly received, an interim increase of about six per cent, to take account of the inflation which had undermined the 1971 award.

As a result of the latest settlement, a constable joins the force at a salary of £1089 a year, rising after six years to £1554; after 17 years' service he gets £1791 a year. Sergeants are paid a maximum of £2037, inspectors £2391 (slightly more in London), chief inspectors get £2700 in the provinces and £2781 in the Metropolitan. Senior officers' pay is currently £3200 for superintendents whilst a London chief superintendent gets £4230. The highest paid policeman in the country, Robert Mark, the Metropolitan Commissioner, gets £14,000. He is followed by the chief constable of Lancashire, with £10,000 and the chief constable of West Yorkshire, just under £10,000. Both these, however, will be paid much less when their forces are drastically reduced by the next wave of force mergers in 1974. Chief constables of the other forces are paid between £4500 and £8500 (in round terms), depending on the populations of their police areas.

Any assessment of police pay must, in fairness, go beyond the basic rates. Every policeman is entitled either to free accommodation or a tax-free rent allowance, which can be as high as £10 a week in London and averages between £6 and £7 in the provinces, although Scottish rates are much lower.

In addition, there is a London lead of £50 for the lower ranks; some forces are paid undermanning allowances of about two pounds a week, and London police, in particular, have substantial regular overtime payments. A constable's £1554 after six years' service in London is equivalent, for a married man receiving maximum rent allowance, to a salary of about £3000 in total pay and allowances. The provincial picture is much less attractive, yet the manpower situation in London remains so serious that at the end of 1971 the Metropolitan branch of the Police Federation was campaigning for a higher rate of pay for the police of the capital.

Inadequate pay is the most often cited reason for police manpower difficulties. A survey on wastage carried out by the Home Office Police Research and Development Branch between 1967 and 1969 found that pay was the major reason given by forty per cent of those who resigned.

The authorities often point to the substantial benefit of free police housing or a generous (and tax-free) rent allowance which, they say, puts the police pay picture in a much better light. They also complain about the high cost of police pensions, caused by the fact that the average police pensioner draws benefit about ten years longer than other employees.

'Our pay is nothing like what it should be,' said a London constable. 'We ought at least to get higher pay for working shifts and weekends.' This is a very popular view with officers who work shifts. It is true that the Royal Commission took such factors into account in 1960, but the policeman knows that trade unions have negotiated much better rates for shift-working in industry.

The manpower shortage has meant that, although the basic working week has been progressively reduced since the war from a six-day, forty-eight-hour week to one of five days and forty hours, forces that are undermanned have required their members to work compulsory overtime. London policemen continued to work a six-day week until 1970, when it was decided that they would get one extra day off every four weeks, the first alteration in working hours in the force since 1910.

In the majority of forces, however, the basic working week is adhered to and opportunities for members to add to their wages through paid overtime are very few. Policemen in London have a small lead in basic pay over the provinces, made up of £50 a year London allowance and a maximum of £65 'undermanning allowance'. This latter is paid to one or two other seriously undermanned forces, but otherwise the principle of a standard rate of pay throughout the service has been maintained. The only substantial variation in incomes is caused by rent allowances, which reflect housing costs in the different police areas.

Whatever the reasons which attract men to the police service, therefore, it is unlikely that many are enticed by the prospect of high wages. Why, then, do they become policemen?

'People are always telling me that they wouldn't have my job for a fortune,' said a London constable. 'Sometimes they say "I don't know how you can do it," as if I was the bloody hangman or something. What do they think we are? There's nothing different about policemen.'

The public, in general, does have a feeling that policemen are indeed 'different'. Small boys may go through a phase of wanting to be policemen when they grow up, but the job comes well down the popularity stakes in any survey of school leavers' anticipations.

The wish for security is still, after twenty-five years of almost full employment and the welfare state, the most potent recruiting ally of the police. At the same time as the survey on wastage mentioned above, the Home Office commissioned a project by the Government Social Survey Department into all aspects of man-management in the service. Three thousand policemen, representative of all ranks, were asked to give their main personal reason for joining the police. Almost half said that they had wanted security. 'Of course I could get more money in a factory,' said an Oxford constable. 'I served my time as an instrument maker. But what with strikes and short time, I'd never know from one week to the next just how much I was going to bring home. That's no good to me.'

Another common reason for joining the police, confirmed by the survey, was that recruits were looking for plenty of job interest and a fair amount of excitement. 'I had two years in an insurance office in the city,' said a young London constable. 'It was the same thing every day. There were fellows in the same room who'd been there nearly forty years, ever since they left school. I used to look at them and wonder if that would be me in a few years' time.'

The survey found that less than one in ten of those interviewed claimed to have had a lifelong ambition to join the police. Other factors which might have been expected to weigh heavily in the choice of a police career scored low marks in the survey. For instance, only five per cent gave as their main reason for joining the fact that the public respects the police and the job has some social status. Only twelve per cent were influenced by the housing provision. Against this, the favourable pension scheme still retains its attractions, with a fifth of those interviewed saying that it was their main reason for joining.

There are two main avenues of entry into the police. The most common is by direct entry as a constable from the age of nineteen. (The recruitment of constables at eighteen is under active consideration.) The other is through the cadet schemes operated by all forces for youths between sixteen and eighteen. The cadets are by far the most significant recent development in police recruiting. Before the war and for a number of years afterwards it was common to find boys employed in police stations as uniformed messengers, with a general understanding that they would become constables when old enough to join. Otherwise, there was no scheme by which the service sought to attract school leavers who might have been interested in a police career. Until national service was discontinued the gap between leaving school and joining the force was at least five years, and is still between three years and four. In some ways the cadet schemes emerged more by accident than design. In London the term 'police cadet' was applied to the boy messengers but they received little formal training and it was found that many of them failed to become satisfactory constables. 'The trouble was,' said a London sergeant, 'that they were simply tea boys, fetching the super's fags and that sort of thing. They had a police uniform and liked to show off in it in front of their mates. At the nick they were called Freddie and Johnnie and they got too cocky. To lads like these, the discipline of the training school was a hell of a shock and then when they got to their stations and found that it was no longer Johnnie but 234 Smith, they couldn't adjust.' This sergeant used to say that not one son of his would ever join the Metropolitan Police; now two of them have been through the cadet scheme at Hendon. The cadet training complex at Hendon is the last word in sophisticated police education. It may have been born out of the recognized failings of the old cadet system, but it owes much to the experience gained by the armed forces with their apprenticeship schemes and its present Commandant was formerly in charge of an army apprentices' school. Boys come in at various stages, depending upon age, but it is acknowledged that the cadet corps can do more with a boy who joins at sixteen than with a later entrant. The full course lasts three years, during which Hendon has every opportunity to mould a youth into a promising police recruit. Hendon pays more attention to a boy's mental and physical needs than to police training. A separate establishment, at Ashford in Kent, provides cadets with opportunities to study for the O-levels and A-levels they missed at school. A cadet is not selected for his academic ability and he is more likely to be the boy who has done quite well at secondary modern or comprehensive school than the outstanding grammar school product.

At one time a number of voices, including the Police Federation, expressed some alarm about the growth of the cadet scheme. It was thought to be dangerous to bring youngsters into a wholly residential police environment because of the danger of producing young constables with a narrow outlook.

An interesting feature of the Hendon scheme is its insistence on separation between cadets and regular policemen. Even when, towards the end of their courses, cadets are detached to police divisions for training purposes, they are still under the control of their own instructors and live together as cadets. 'The longer we have a boy as a cadet, the more we can make of him,' a senior instructor at Hendon told me, 'and this means keeping him all the time under our jurisdiction.'

The cadet scheme gives the police an opportunity to avoid making mistakes. Throughout the training programme there is a constant weeding-out system which eliminates the boy who is clearly unsuitable. Due allowances are made for age and maturity, but as the time for appointment to the force draws nearer more attention is paid to the borderline case. This may be one of the reasons why wastage among young policemen who have joined the force after cadet service is notably lower than with other entrants.

Every effort is made to broaden a cadet's outlook. He is expected to undertake some form of voluntary service in the community and many Metropolitan cadets work in youth clubs or help old people. Others work in hospitals and with mentally handicapped children. 'I could put up a notice asking for volunteers for hospital work now,' the senior instructor said, 'and it would be filled with names in no time at all. The important thing is that the boys do not volunteer because it is the right thing to do, but because they genuinely want to help other people.'

Some policemen suspect that the cadet scheme aims to produce an officer-class within the force. 'We never try to create the feeling in a cadet that he belongs to an elite body in the force,' said the senior instructor, 'although of course we encourage a competitive spirit between the cadets. It is the Metropolitan Police which is the elite body, not the cadet corps.'

Many Metropolitan cadets are the sons of provincial policemen whose fathers have told them that this is the force with the career opportunities. The Metropolitan cadet scheme has prospered because of its size and the vast amount of money available to the force. With over five hundred cadets under training, the force has established a solid basis for recruiting and in 1970 gained over a third of its new men from this source.

There are altogether some three thousand cadets in England and Wales. The standard of local cadet schemes tends to vary in relation to the size of each force. It is to be regretted that provincial chief constables have not been prepared to organize cadet schemes on a regional basis, preferring to maintain their own cadet corps. None of these is as comprehensive as the Metropolitan scheme.

Youngsters become police cadets for a variety of reasons. The boy from the secondary modern school, without much in the way of examination results to offer an employer, sees in the cadets an opening for a definite career. Others are attracted by the smart uniform and the obvious comradeship which exists. Here the cadet himself is a potent factor in encouraging his friends to apply. The police cadet scheme offers a boy many of the advantages of army life without the disadvantage of being posted far from home or the requirement to serve for a given number of years. Some come in because they have always wanted to be policemen and they like the prospect of a glamorous occupation.

The effect of ex-cadet entry into the force has been shown at the academic level. Whereas in 1960 the Royal Commission on the Police was disturbed about the low educational standard of police recruits, many ex-cadets have O-level and A-level passes which put a much healthier tint on what would otherwise be a fairly depressing picture.

Whatever their merits, however, the cadet schemes cannot supply more than between a third and a half of all entrants to the service. In any case, a police force which recruited entirely from this source would soon become totally unrepresentative of the community it served. It is generally accepted that the service should be composed of a wide cross-section of the nation, but it is arguable that this is not a practical possibility. 'The police service cannot hope to compete with industry for the best brains of the country,' said a chief constable, 'and at the moment it is hard-pressed to secure a reasonable share of the ordinary intelligent young men.'

In the sixties, the chief constable of Durham, Mr Alec Muir, caused a lot of trouble within the service by asserting that, at a time when criminals were becoming more intelligent, the police were becoming less so. Muir wanted more contact between the police and universities, including a degree course in police sciences, and the restriction of appointments to the rank of superintendent and above to police officers who held degrees. A year or two earlier the Royal Commission had pointed out that not one graduate had joined the force in recent years.

In spite of a slow but steady improvement in the educational background of police recruits over the last five years, the fact remains that the average police recruit is unlikely to have stayed at school beyond the minimum leaving age and to have had much further education. As I have pointed out above, the cadet intake tends to improve the general picture, but the level of direct entry remains academically low. It is doubtful if it has even kept pace with the general improvement in educational standards throughout the country. 'It's easy to become a policeman today,' said a recruiting inspector, 'in fact, it's too bloody easy, and that's the trouble.'

It is a fact that almost half of the applications which every police force receives are rejected because the educational standard of the candidates is below even the modest demands of the police. All that a recruit needs to do is to satisfy the force that he has a reasonable ability to read and write. A typical force examination would require him to write a short essay on a topic such as 'Why I want to be a policeman', take a few sentences of dictation, do some elementary arithmetic, and complete a general knowledge test. 'We're not looking for budding schoolmasters,' said a chief constable. 'There is no real need to have a difficult entrance examination for a job which requires more common sense than academic ability.'

The Royal Commission recommended, in 1962, that all forces should give the same test, which should be similar to the simple vocabulary test given in industry and by the army. The Commission said that there could be no absolute pass level for such a test, as chief constables who found recruiting abnormally difficult would have to accept a lower level. They said that it would be 'irresponsible' to set a high educational standard for police entrants when, because of full employment, there would be no hope of maintaining it. No recruitment policy, they said, would be satisfactory until it secured an adequate number of police and also 'sufficient young men of such ability and educational attainment as would fit them to occupy in due course the highest posts in the service'. Obviously, this second objective was not going to be achieved by the simple vocabulary test proposed by the Royal Commission, but they refrained from making positive recommendations on how to attain better-educated young men to fill the higher posts because, at that time, another committee was examining the question of higher training within the police.

It would be wrong to suggest that, because most police recruits have only the minimum of education, the force is necessarily less intelligent than it used to be. Later on, I shall be discussing the very real and encouraging achievements of the Police College, where young officers recruited in the normal way have been remarkably successful both in their performance at the college and afterwards at university. Modern police work does require a high standard of intelligence and in general the force has few shortcomings in this direction. It is true, however, that men who have only

just managed to pass a simple entrance examination are
unlikely, in their subsequent police careers, to succeed in
passing the rigorous promotion examinations, so that many
recruits are destined to remain constables for the whole of
their service.

Apart from the simple educational requirements, the force
stipulates that candidates must satisfy certain physical
standards. The minimum height standard of five feet eight
inches is often criticized. It is said that it is ridiculous to
exclude an otherwise entirely suitable applicant because he is
less than this height. The requirement is based on a belief
that a constable needs to have a physical presence to support
his legal and moral authority. It is not a very convincing
argument, even when supported by no less an expert than the
late Sir Joseph Simpson, the former commissioner of the
Metropolitan Police. He told the Royal Commission that his
shorter officers seemed to have more difficulty in their
dealings with the public, and tended to make up for their
lack of height with a more aggressive approach. At times, the
height question assumes a ridiculous aspect. The City of
London force, in spite of a substantial strength deficiency,
insists on a minimum height of five feet eleven inches.

The other qualification asked of a police recruit is that he
should be of good previous character. 'There's an element of
hit and miss about that,' said a senior officer in Lancashire.
'If the recruit comes from another area, we have to rely on
the local force to carry out the character enquiry. We always
take up the references which he has to supply, but the man
wouldn't give us their names if they knew anything bad
about him.' The character enquiry does its best to trace the
full story of a candidate's previous history, but as it is
conducted by a busy policeman with many other tasks to
perform, it cannot be as thorough as would seem desirable
for a post that puts such stress on personal integrity.

The success or failure of an application to join the force
hinges upon the personal interview between the candidate
and the local chief constable or, in the Metropolitan, the

recruiting board of senior officers. Although chief officers and recruiting boards gain considerable experience of interviews, the possibility that a good candidate may be rejected because of an unfortunate and misleading performance must be very high, just as it is obvious that some men are accepted whose appointment turns out to have been a serious error. Senior officers will admit that the present recruiting system is far from satisfactory. 'The ideal would be a very leisurely but extremely painstaking process in which we had a chance to put a recruit under a microscope,' said a chief constable. 'It just isn't on, and we have to do the best we can. The service cannot afford to be too sophisticated in its selection techniques. There isn't all that much to select.'

A chief constable who admitted in public that his force had deliberately lowered its standards of entry would be in an embarrassing position. Such a statement would reflect on the men in his command. Most chief constables will go no further than stating that police pay is too low to attract enough recruits of the 'right calibre'. It may be significant that in the man-management survey the senior officers who were interviewed were equally divided into those who thought that the right kind of man was being recruited into the service and those who thought that he was not.

A comparison of today's policemen with their predecessors is a difficult exercise. Before the war, nearly every recruit came into the force in the expectation of a job for the next thirty years. The successful candidates were for the most part solid, reliable and fairly unimaginative men. Most of them had no great expectations of promotion, which was in any event a painfully slow business, and they were fully prepared to be constables for the greater part of their service. The high turnover in personnel today means that the nature of the job has changed from being a permanent career to an occupation which many men follow for a number of years before trying something else. The situation might change again if the country were to face a long period of high unemployment and a reduction in the number of alternative jobs open to policemen who are not committed to the career. Some senior officers will say, at least in private and with a touch of nostalgia for the past, that only in such a climate would the police solve their manpower problems.

One possible advantage of a more scientific system of selecting recruits would be the chance of eliminating the man who is psychologically unsuitable for the position of a policeman. By its very nature, police work must sometimes attract the man who wants the power and authority that go with the job. 'This type isn't easy to detect when he applies,' said a chief constable. 'He may seem, on the face of things, to be just the man we are looking for. If a policeman sees his job only in terms of prosecuting offenders to the letter of the law, he may lack the judgement which a policeman must have. Worse still, there is no way of detecting the man who might use his uniform as a cloak for violence.'

The fact that all police probationers can be dismissed at any time within their first two years, on the grounds that they are not likely to become efficient policemen, is a useful safeguard for the service. It gives senior officers an opportunity of remedying their own selection mistakes, although there are times when the facility for sacking a probationer appears to be used in the wrong way, and the unfortunate victim has no avenue of appeal against a dismissal that appears to be arbitrary and unfair.

The majority of police recruits are very young. In 1964 an attempt was made to attract more mature entrants by offering an advanced rate of pay to those aged twenty-two and over, but this was unsuccessful and the scheme was abandoned at the pay settlement in 1971. One source which the authorities had in mind was the man in his late twenties and early thirties who was completing a regular engagement in the armed forces. 'The regular army was once our best source,' said a chief constable. 'We got the ideal type of constable from them, but not any more. They would like to join, because the police offers them the nearest thing in civilian life to what they have been used to in the forces. But nowadays they are more likely to be skilled technicians. Some tell us straight that they couldn't afford to take a big drop in income to start as police recruits and in any case they can get far more in industry.'

Over half the 5,794 men recruited in England and Wales in 1970 were nineteen years old, including 1,500 cadets. Just over 2,500 recruits were aged twenty-two and over, with the greatest concentration at the lower age point.

'We offer a recruit just about a thousand a year,' said a recruiting officer. 'Actually its rather more if you take account of housing and opportunities for overtime, which are good in this force.'

It is only recently that the police have gone in for elaborate advertising campaigns for recruits. The budget is still only a fraction of what the armed forces spend and a police campaign can have nothing like the impact and mass coverage which they achieve. Police recruiting advertisements have tended to concentrate on the public service aspect of police work and emphasize the worthwhile nature of an important job, full of interest and excitement. The approach has been something of a cross between the 'join the professionals' slogan of the army and the more staid, status-conscious appeal of a banking house.

The efforts made over the past five years to attract graduates, in a bid to secure the men with the potential to make rapid progress to the top, have been an unhappy failure. The advertising in the quality papers has been very good. but the appeal of the graduate entry scheme (see Chapter Five) has been minimal simply because it is based on a rigid requirement that even graduates must complete a minimum of two years as constables. In fact, a graduate who comes in under the scheme is being offered an almost cast-iron guarantee of being promoted to inspector within five years. In 1970, only about a hundred graduates applied for consideration and of these only nine were considered suitable, of whom four were already serving as constables. This is in spite of the fact that a superintendent is attached to the Home Office with a specific brief to encourage graduate recruitment.

The service is, as a body, completely unmoved by the failure of the graduate entry scheme. Policemen recall the bitter experiences of the inter-war years when Lord Trenchard attempted to introduce an officer-class in the force. Whatever improvements can be made to the present recruiting system it seems certain that nothing will be done which will alter the policeman's own insistence that every recruit must start from the bottom. The archetypal police recruit, therefore, is still going to be either an ex-cadet or a young, not very academically minded man looking for a job with considerable security and more than its share of interest and possible excitement.

3 The young policeman

One of the most remarkable things about the British police service is its youth. Of some seventy thousand constables serving in England and Wales in 1970, roughly half were under thirty. At the other end of the age scale, only twelve hundred constables were over fifty, and most of these were ready to retire. The service is young because of two factors: the comparatively short career span obliges the great majority to retire in their early fifties; and the high turnover rate since the war means that fewer men remain in the force to complete pensionable service. 'We have to send out boys to do men's work,' said a senior officer in the West End of London. 'If we stop to think about it, the responsibility which we load on their shoulders is frightening.'

It seems odd, therefore, that one common complaint against the police is that they are out of touch with the young. Go into any section house for single men in the Metropolitan Police, for instance, and the atmosphere is not very different from what one would expect in any other hostel for young people, say a students' hall or an apprentices' lodging. The music on the record player will be from the top twenty, the clothes worn off duty will be the same as those favoured by other young men of the same age. Even the hair styles will not be all that different.

Older policemen shake their heads about the type of youngster coming into the force. Chief officers issue discreet instructions to sergeants and inspectors about beards and side whiskers, and the length of hair visible beneath a helmet. Although extra-long hair looks out of place with a police uniform, it is a good thing that the service relaxed its rigid 'short back and sides' rule of a few years back. A young constable cannot be cut off entirely from the pop society, in spite of the conflict which arises when he is confronted with some aspects of it. Not without misgivings at the top, the police have been forced by their manpower problem to make concessions in this direction which, only a few years ago, would have been unthinkable.

When national service ended, a new type of recruit came into the police. After recruiting for so many years almost exclusively from the forces, or from men who had completed national service, the police began accepting nineteen-year-olds. These were the young men who changed the police service's traditional ideas about how a policeman should look in uniform, how he should dress in his own clothes, what he could and could not do in his own time. Not that the traditionalists gave in willingly. Some ten years ago, for example, a young Metropolitan constable on duty at Buckingham Palace shocked his superiors by growing a beard. Perhaps he was bored with standing for hours outside a gate in a wall. 'Shave it off,' came the order. 'I won't,' was the reply. A discipline board dismissed the constable for disobeying orders. He appealed to the Home Secretary and won his case, a victory which was taken as tacit consent for other policemen to grow beards. The young policeman who came into the force straight from civilian life, who had never stood to attention and saluted a superior in his life, had quite different ideas about discipline from his predecessors. He simply refused to be pushed around. In time, the service adjusted its own attitudes and supervisory officers began to learn that they would have to handle men in a more enlightened manner. Not all policemen approve of the changed climate of tolerance which is so evident today. They remember their own days as recruits, when the man who insisted on being different and asserting his own personality would not have lasted very long.

To an older generation of serving policemen, the casual attitude to discipline which they detect in the younger officer is evidence of declining standards. 'We used to recruit men,' said a Yorkshire sergeant who served in the Welsh Guards, and still carried himself like the RSM he had been, 'now we get boys. Stopping national service was the worst thing this country ever did.'

It would be news to many young policemen to learn that they enjoy a much more liberal regime these days. Many policemen still resign because of the multitude of petty pinpricks which they encounter every day, and what they regard as the oppressiveness of sergeants and senior officers. 'I put in a short report on a woman who'd collapsed in the street,' said one young probationer. 'Do you know how many times it came back to me? Four. Piffling little queries like had I spelt the surname correct, why was the report a day late, and so on. It gets you down.'

Young policemen today are more ready to question what they regard as unnecessary restrictions and pettifogging supervision. In the first few months of his probation period a recruit finds himself in a somewhat artificial world. At training school he is working alongside other new entrants and his experience of older policemen and senior officers is confined to his instructors. His main concern is with the theory of police work and the training schools do not provide him with an insight into the life he is to lead in his force. For some young constables the contrast between the helpful sergeant instructor at the training school and the patrol sergeant at the first station can come as a shock. 'It would be wonderful if every sergeant in charge of constables was a born leader with the knack of bringing the best out of recruits,' said a superintendent, 'but obviously there are big differences. A good sergeant can do wonders for recruits, but a bad one can make the difference between a lad deciding to stick it out or resign.'

When there is talk about conflict between the police and the young, there is a need to be more specific. How many young people feel that the police are their natural enemies? The public appears to be conditioned into believing that everyone under twenty-five fits into one of the categories to which all young people must belong: they either smoke pot, demonstrate, fornicate, or wreck football trains. Worse still, they are students. The fact that the great majority of young people do none of these things does not seem to have registered with public opinion. The true situation is that many young people today are hardly more likely to come into personal conflict with the police than any previous generation did. What has intensified is the conflict between a sizeable minority of the young and the values that the police uphold.

The young, for instance, have the drug scene almost entirely to themselves. At least until the Industrial Relations Bill brought thousands of trade unionists on to the streets in 1971, it was mainly the young who walked from Aldermaston, besieged Grosvenor Square, and occupied colleges. Vandalism, another major police problem, is largely an activity of the young, just as it is the young motor cyclist, breaking all the traffic laws ever made, who conducts a constant running battle with police patrols. In all these activities, young people very soon come up against the first line of the establishment's defences, the uniformed policeman. Often, very often, the young demonstrator, junkie, tearaway or Hell's Angel faces a policeman of virtually his own age. They represent two worlds a generation apart and totally opposed, but if the young offender is an obvious misfit in society, so to some extent is the young policeman, set apart from his own generation and obliged to enforce the requirements of an older one.

The young policeman senses the conflict. He can see things in the same light as other young people but he knows that it is not for him to start making concessions or to attempt to compromise between the demands of his job and the problems of his own generation. Sometimes the conflict arises out of the local environment. Only recently, for example, have the planning experts begun to take stock of the major errors they perpetrated in the creation of most new towns in Britain.

A young constable faces a critical point in his career when, after completing his recruit training and having worked for a short period in the company of other policemen, he begins to go out alone. 'It's not easy for a lad of nineteen to face down a gang of youths on a street corner,' said an inspector whose children were older than most of the constables in his town section. 'I can just stop, put my head out of the car window, and tell them to get off home. They'll take it from me because they know me, because I'm old enough to be their father, and because they know I'm an inspector. But they see a boy doing his best to look like a big man and it's a chance to take the mickey out of the police. If the PC is six foot with the shoulders to go with it, he's all right, because he looks like trouble. But if he's a bare five nine and ten stones wet through, they might try to take him on.'

This inspector suggested that some young policemen resigned when they had found themselves in this situation and had, for the first time, realized that a policeman needed guts. 'They would never say that they left because they were scared, but it happens.' A PC in a Somerset town decided that he had stood as much as a self-respecting policeman ought to stand from one street-corner gang. He invited the ringleader round a corner and they fought. The youth lost and his mother complained. The policeman appeared before the chief constable and was fined for discreditable conduct. A chief constable with any appreciation of what young policemen sometimes face would have earmarked that man for early promotion. The police operate within the strict limitations of the law, and nowadays, the public is much more aware of the extent of police powers. This creates difficulties for the younger constables which more experienced policemen, by careful use of the 'ways and means act', avoid. 'You go up to a lot of yobs outside a coffee bar, revving up their motorbikes and tell them to clear off,' said a young constable in North London. 'Ten to one there is big-mouth knowall who'll say you can't make him move on.

That's when you start checking licences and insurance and making it as difficult for them as you can. You can fill a book with the offences these kids commit on motorbikes. If they start taking the mickey, there's a law to fit.'

Some young constables, feeling themselves insecure because of their inexperience, have found to their cost that a friendly approach to people of their own age can be a mistake.

'We had a lad here', said an ex-cadet, 'straight from training school. One night the sergeant's walking round the beat with him and there was a gang on the corner with a couple of girls. As soon as they saw him they started calling, "Goodnight Barry." The sergeant went mad.' Constables in training are reminded constantly that they represent the entire police force. To a policeman, dignity is all important, and loss of face in an encounter with the irreverent young is unthinkable.

If the police are ever to improve their standing with those sections of the younger generation which give them trouble, it is more likely to come from the efforts of young policemen themselves, rather than because of a public-relations exercise mounted by authority. All the lectures to youth clubs with frank discussions over tea and buns will pass the hooligan by, because he would not be found dead inside a youth club. This is a major area of police activity where the young policeman has got to abandon his 'man apart' role and establish close understanding with people of his own age; not for the sake of improving the 'image', but because more and more the need for contact arises. In the drug area, for instance, the wide extension of police powers may have led to a big increase in the number of convictions, but it is doubtful if the law has had any significant effect on efforts to persuade the young of the dangers involved.

In a Midlands city a few years ago, a doctor in charge of a hospital addiction unit discovered that he had a drug problem on his hands. Simply because there was no one else to treat addicts, he had to do what he could. The doctor asked the police for help. They began by tackling the sources of supply, which were quite open. Local chemists were making up drug prescriptions issued by doctors who were either naive or something much worse. Thanks to the local level of understanding between the police and the doctor, what might have become a major police worry has been contained. One of the reasons for this was that the police had the good sense to allow a young constable on the vice squad to frequent the haunts of the few known addicts, where he was able to put some of the youngsters involved in touch with the addiction unit before it was too late. In one sense, the police were lucky because of the absence of a black market in drugs, but the way it was handled illustrated the usefulness of allowing a young policeman to work on his own initiative, even if in a highly unorthodox fashion. Significantly, too, the police action was directed towards prevention, not prosecution.

'After Mick Jagger was raided the second time,' said a London constable, 'we could sense real resentment from the kids in the discotheques. It wasn't hero worship of Jagger, just a feeling that the police were trying to get him because of who he was. You just can't convince intelligent youngsters that cannabis is dangerous, and if the truth were told I doubt if you'd find many policemen who knew what they were talking about, even though they think it is. But there's a law, so we carry it out.'

Here is an area of conflict where it appears that something can be done to ease tensions. The drug problem, besides being the most recent, is potentially the most dangerous. It is almost exclusively a problem of the young and is inextricably linked with the pop scene and notions of rebellion. Authority's answer has been to strengthen the law and ask the police to bear the main burden of combating its growth. The weakness of this approach is that the intelligent young resent a law which seems to them to be based upon an unfounded assumption that cannabis is addictive, and intense police activity in enforcing the law merely strengthens their hostility. Such bodies as the National Council for Civil

Liberties allege that the police operate the drug laws in a manner which discriminates against young people. 'Of course we stop mostly young people,' said a London constable on a drugs squad. 'You don't go up to a man in a bowler hat and say, "Excuse me, but do you happen to have a joint on you?" You go up to a long-haired hippie with peep sandals and filthy feet and turn him over. We find drugs because we know where to look for them.'

It could be true that individual constables find the added powers of the drugs law helpful in dealing with itinerant young people, if only because they provide the legal excuse to stop and search. 'I've turned quite a few over for drugs,' said another London constable, 'but nowadays you're damned lucky to find any because they've got wise to it. But you'd be surprised how often you find them with stolen property, or they turn out to be wanted for something.'

The fact that cannabis and amphetamines have 'caught on' with the young sometimes places a young policeman in difficulties of a personal kind. A young constable in a northern force said 'I used to go to a discotheque quite a lot with my girl friend. Before we got hot on drugs round here it was all right. But there was a raid one night when we were there, looking for cannabis. They didn't find any, but I had an interview with an inspector. The inspector asked me about cannabis and why I hadn't noticed it or reported it, because the other police had. I told him I knew nothing about it, but I don't think he believed it.'

The immediate consequences of the raid, for this young constable, were that he began to wonder if his personal file contained a black mark (probably it did), he lost his girl friend because her friends suspected him of informing, and he knew that he would never be welcome at that place again. 'You can't have ordinary mates when you're a copper,' said a young policeman in a London section house. 'I used to belong to a pretty good youth club and I was in the soccer team. It wasn't so bad when I was a cadet because I was at Hendon and if they started getting on at me at the club about how the police picked on kids, I'd just say, "Don't look at me". But now I'm wearing a helmet they don't want to know me.'

In London, nearly every young single policeman lives in a police section house. These are distributed over the Metropolitan Police area and one advantage to the force is that they provide large concentrations of men who can, if the need arises, be called out immediately. The section houses date from the Trenchard era. (He insisted that the waiters in the dining rooms should wear dinner jackets.) The early ones were austere barracks, but lately the force has been trying to improve amenities and the modern ones offer a good standard of accommodation. In the boroughs, most single men live at home, but others, and those in the counties, find problems with lodgings. A single constable gets half a married man's rent allowance to assist with his lodging costs, but seaside and university areas pose special difficulties. 'Landladies prefer students,' said one young constable in Oxford, 'because it works out more profitable to have a student in for the short terms than have a policeman all the year round.'

'Police widows are best,' said one veteran of half a dozen lodgings, 'if you don't mind being mothered and told how their husbands used to do your job. They expect you to be on nights and they don't think twice about making sandwiches. Other landladies always moan and say they can't afford it on what you're paying them.'

In a brand-new and quite luxurious hostel for single policemen in the Midlands, I found one resident who wanted to go back to lodgings. 'They've got everything here,' he admitted, 'but it's not like being in a home, it's an institution and you get the feeling that you're never off the job.'

In the Metropolitan, some young men resent the rules of the section houses, particularly the ban on women in the rooms, but the majority recognize the need for some regulations to ensure the comfort of others. 'If half the lads have to be up at five in the morning,' said a warden, 'we can't have the others making a row at midnight.' The force does permit older single men to move out of the section houses into their own property. 'I'll get out of here at the first opportunity,' said a man at a Kennington section house. 'This place is a cross between the Salvation Army and the Union Jack club.' This, incidentally, is not the view given by the leading character in the Metropolitan recruiting film, *Policeman*, who is shown in his single bedroom in a West End section house. 'Just like a hotel,' he says. 'What would this cost me in London?'

Naturally, many young policemen marry policewomen. 'I used to say that they only joined to find a husband,' said one of these, 'and I used to laugh at the others for going out with them. Then I did it myself.'

'I'm always pleased when a young policeman say's he's getting married,' said the chief constable quoted above. 'It's a sign that he's ready to settle down and take on more responsibilities. A young single man has plenty of money and he wants his fun. That's when he might do something stupid and get the sack. If he's married, he's at home with his wife.' But the same chief constable agreed that some young constables rushed into marriage and found themselves beset with problems. 'We can offer a married man a police house almost straight away. I'd like them all to start off in police property and buy their own home when they can really afford to, but most of them want to get their hands on the full rent allowance straight away. You can't blame them. It certainly is a good help with the mortgage. What they don't realize is that the wife stops working as soon as the first child comes along. Then they have to manage on a young constable's pay and meet the mortgage and the rates and the hire purchase and everything else. I know that everyone else does too. But policemen must on no account get into debt. You'd be surprised how many of them get in above their necks and have to get a loan from our benevolent fund. Their wives can't manage properly or they've bitten off more than they can chew.'

Young policemen are not immune from the acquisitive side of affluence. They sometimes find that a constable's modest starting pay cuts them off from the possessions which other young men of their age enjoy. This is more true in the case of the married man, for one of the problems at Metropolitan section houses is parking space for residents' cars. The young married policeman, however, has to adjust to the financial problems of matrimony, particularly when his wife stops working.

A senior officer in London said, 'I always ask a man who wants a loan from the benevolent fund if he has a car. Of course he usually has and I suggest that he sells it. But they think a car is essential. I was forty before I owned one, but young couples nowadays want everything at once and policemen are no exception.'

A Metropolitan constable with a long experience of welfare problems said, 'I can never understand why the young ones always seem to try every other way of getting money before they come to our own funds. Sometimes they've been to moneylenders and when we check they are paying nearly fifty per cent interest and are taking out further loans to pay back on the first.' Only a small proportion of policemen get into debt in this way, but the worry of being in debt is only increased when a man knows that it is an offence against the Discipline Code.

With most provincial forces working a five-day week, opportunities for earning extra money through overtime are restricted to the badly undermanned forces. The Police Federation has always insisted that its demand for a reduced working week, which has led to the five-day week, was a genuine quest for extra leisure, not a disguised pay claim. This is often said by other trade unions, but the pattern in industry today is that overtime is looked on as a right. 'What's the good of having an extra day off once a fortnight,' said one young policeman, 'if you can't afford to spend anything? Give me the overtime every time.'

Pressure from disgruntled wives, and sometimes from girl friends, accounts for many early resignations. The financial problem of managing on one small basic wage is obvious, but

other reasons which make wives dislike the force are the shift
work which plays havoc with social life, and the restraint
which being a policeman imposes on private affairs. This is
felt as much by the policeman's wife who has a job herself. A
Kent police wife, married a year, said, 'I'm often surprised
that he is still in the force. After we married I thought I
would go mad if he didn't stop talking shop. His only friends
are other policemen and my friends are nearly all police
wives. The police widow earns her pension, believe me,
because she does thirty years in the force just the same as he
does.' One senior officer told me that in these days when so
many young policemen were married it was essential that
their seniors kept a close watch on them. He told me of one
case in which a young married policeman began attracting
adverse reports about his work. 'He was coming up for the
time when I had to decide whether to recommend his
appointment should be confirmed after his probation. His
inspector and sergeant both said that from a good beginning
he'd become bone idle. I had a long chat and I could not find
out any reason for it. He insisted that everything was all right
at home. Then, quite by chance, my wife met his wife and
found out that she was under the doctor for nerves. She was
frightened of being alone at nights and wanted him to resign.
I put him on a day job for a couple of months and persuaded
him to move into a police flat where there were two other
police families in the same block. He's never looked back
since.' As this officer pointed out, there were limits to what
could be done in this direction and many young policemen
would resent interference in their personal affairs, no matter
how well-intentioned it was, but the police authorities are
well aware of the need for paying close attention to welfare
problems. In many forces, the suggestion made by the Police
Advisory Board's working party on management in 1966 that
civilian welfare officers should be appointed has been acted
on. Unfortunately, in some cases, the man appointed is a
former senior officer in the force. 'Ours is an ex-senior
officer,' said one young constable, 'and believe me it was the

way he went about things that caused most of the trouble in the force. Now they expect me to take my troubles to him. They must be joking.'

Other forces could benefit from a little enlightenment in the way they handle young constables. A young constable in Dorset married a policewoman who belonged to the Bournemouth borough force. The two forces were merged but, under the regulations, the policewoman was protected against compulsory transfer outside the borough. As soon as they were married, the chief constable transferred the husband to Weymouth, some thirty miles away. The wife refused to be moved, but the husband had to go. The chief constable argued that he was offering the young couple a nice police house in a pleasant town, although there was a spare house in Bournemouth. Both applied for a transfer to another force.

The service is right to be paying more and more attention to man-management, and in a later chapter I will be dealing with this aspect of police life. It is, however, in its treatment of its younger members that the service can make positive improvements in its high wastage rates. In the undermanned forces, in spite of all the attention paid to basic training, senior officers will admit that the young recruit is often exposed to situations which demand more experience than he has got. 'In the old days we brought them along much more slowly,' said a patrol inspector. 'We could keep them with the senior constables and make sure that there were not too many probationers on one shift. That's the traditional way, but nowadays they aren't out of training school five minutes before they are showing another recruit the ropes.' It is often the young constable who bears much of the increased work load which has come on to the police in recent years.

The personal radio has been one reason for the increase in the number of incidents which an individual beat man will be expected to handle. Yet it has also helped the supervisory officer by providing a contact between the man on the scene and the station. 'I can't think how we used to manage before we had radio,' said a sergeant, 'I'm always drilling it into them to call in, call in, all the time. On a busy Saturday night when it gets to chucking-out time I can feel my palms starting to sweat. These lads are dealing with half a dozen jobs at once and you've only got half the picture in the station. Before we had radio they went out on duty and no one in the station had to bother. If they needed help, they had to ring in from a police pillar or hope that some taxi driver would give them a hand. Now they use the station as their extra hand, but what you get is a message to say they've gone to a fight, and you keep trying to find out what's happening. You must know if you should send a car, that's if they aren't all occupied already.'

One cannot be in the company of working policemen for long without being aware that this is a job where the majority of men take a fierce, if not often articulate, pride in their calling. Young policemen, react, if anything, more strongly to ill-informed criticism than the veterans who have heard it all before. 'The thing that annoys me,' said a young London constable, 'is when someone gets up in Parliament and talks about policemen not being educated. They give the impression that we are all thick coppers with no education. I'd like to take some MPs round Brixton with me any night of the week. That's the education a policeman gets.'

Whether some senior officers make sufficient allowances for the lack of maturity of young policemen is open to argument. If an older constable is the subject of a complaint, his experience may help him to adopt a philosophical attitude to the lengthy rigmarole laid down for investigating allegations, but the younger man, finding himself up against the regulations for the first time, may be alarmed and resentful, or wonder whose side his senior officers are on. 'I've had one complaint to answer so far,' said a City of London constable, 'and it was so bloody silly. I booked a taxi driver who turned out to be Jewish. Without thinking I asked him for his Christian names. He went bonkers.'

If young recruits set out on their careers with romantic notions of the excitement of police work, they soon come across the sordid side of everyday life.

'I remember my first sudden death,' said a probationer. 'It was the first time I'd ever seen a dead body. She was an old woman who lived alone with her dog. When we broke in she'd been dead nearly four weeks — nearly four weeks — and the corpse was blown up like an air mattress. You should have smelled it, it was awful. And the dog had starved to death beside her.'

In October 1970 there was much publicity about the young Salford policeman who had the job of telling a husband and wife that their small child had been killed in a gassing tragedy in Blackpool. Not only had he broken the news as gently as possible, but he had driven the couple to Blackpool in his own car after his night duty. This incident was remarkable only in the amount of comment it attracted, for it is the young constable on the beat who, by the very nature of his job, often becomes the one who has to take bad news to the home. 'Some old people get the same feeling of shock on seeing a policeman on the doorstep,' said a Birmingham constable, 'as they used to have about telegraph boys. It's a job we hate doing, telling relatives about sudden deaths, but who else is there? The hospitals ring up, or we get a message from another force, and we have to go and knock on the door. There was a fatal accident at Walsall once, and they needed the wife to go to identify the body. He was a commercial traveller and when I got to the house it was a woman with two small kids and they were getting ready for a birthday party.'

'I had to tell a woman that her husband had been killed in an accident at work,' said a Lancashire officer, 'he'd fallen off a catwalk forty feet up. When I went it was a woman in a wheelchair. She'd had polio for twenty years and there was no one else, no kids and no relatives. What's more she had a weak heart. What gets me is that the factory knew this, and they never said a word. I suppose they were frightened that we'd ask someone there to tell her.'

Every constable must have a store of such incidents in his

mind. He sees the different reactions of all manner of people to the impact of the unexpected family disaster and experience teaches him when a cup of tea or the sympathy of a woman neighbour is required and when it is better simply to leave them alone with their grief. It is nearly twenty years since I knocked on a door to tell a woman with two small children that her husband, who had gone away that morning to hunt for a job in Manchester, had collapsed and died in the train. Of the hundreds of things that happen to a policeman during his years on the beat, these are the ones that remain in the memory.

There can be no set pattern of training to teach policemen how to be kind. Each officer will respond to human emotions in his own way. The odd thing is that every policeman seems to be the right man to deal with the family situation, whatever it is. 'I will never forget two young policemen who went to my brother's house when he hanged himself in the garage,' said an elderly Harrow man. 'It was so unexpected, he didn't seem to have a care in the world, but one morning the milkman found him and called the police. My mother was over seventy then, and she didn't know anything was wrong until the police called. They never told her that he had committed suicide, only that he had died suddenly. She never found out what had happened, simply because two young men realized that the shock would have killed her as well. To tell you the truth, I'd never thought much of the police before that happened.'

What every young policeman does know is that the force attaches great importance to maintaining good relations with the public. It is the constant theme of so many of the lectures he gets during his training. 'I wish there were lectures for members of the public on how to treat the police,' said one constable, 'I'm serious. As far as we are concerned, any dirty job that needs doing has got to be done, and they take it for granted that we'll do it. Then why do they stand by and watch when you need their help for a change?' This officer had been called to remove a noisy drunk from a bus station one Saturday night. He finished up fighting the man and his two sober companions whilst hundreds of spectators looked on. A Lancashire policewoman was badly assaulted when she tried to arrest a man who had stolen goods from a supermarket. 'We were rolling around in the gutter and there must have been a hundred people watching. Some of the women were shouting at the man but nobody did a thing. Then I felt him dragged away from me and it was a little old taxi driver that we were always booking for touting. "I'll hold him, love," he said, "your eye shadow looks a bit of a mess".'

Being a young policeman on the beat means knowing how to deal with the eccentrics and others who become the local characters of any neighbourhood. 'A lot of crazy people,' said one constable, 'seem to have this thing about electricity. They'll ring the station and tell you that the bloke next door has rigged up a machine to send electrical impulses through them. You'd be surprised how many there are like that.'

Occasionally, the young policeman comes across the pathetic examples of human degradation for which the welfare state has little answer. 'We broke into one house with a bailiff and a mental health officer,' said one constable, 'I think it was because of the rates. It was a big terrace house which would make four flats nowadays, with just this one woman living in it. She must have lived there on her own since her father died. You've never seen anything like it. We waded through piles of rubbish in every room, literally as high as your knees. Newspapers from twenty years back, tin cans, bottles, everything. There was no light or heating and no water. She'd lived like that all those years, just drawing on her father's money. Every night she'd gone rooting through dustbins to bring stuff back to pile up in the house with the rest. She was verminous, yet neighbours had given her meals. You'd at least think that the bank would have done something, wouldn't you? She'd been a customer all those years, and her father was a big builder at one time. But when the money ran out, they just told her not to come in any more.'

Younger police officers, men and women, are specially suitable for the preventive role played by the police in the field of juvenile crime. Whilst older officers can fill the 'father figure' position in these bureaux, it is the younger officer who is more likely to be attuned to the young people who are dealt with by police juvenile liaison schemes, which rely upon cautioning and supervision of young offenders as an alternative to prosecution. Surprisingly, this aspect of the police role is not always looked upon with favour by magistrates and probation officers. A young northern officer on juvenile liaison work said, 'Some probation officers don't like what we're doing. They say it's wrong to put a kid under police supervision without a court case, but we think we can help these children without giving them a criminal record. What really upsets the probation officer is that we can do the job better than he can. You know why? Because they're just a little bit frightened of us, that's why, and they think the probation officer is the chap they go to when they've been let off in court. I wouldn't do their job for twice my money. Thankless, it must be.'

Young policemen soon become older policemen. In a sense, their first two years have something of an artificial flavour, because the accent is on training, supervision, and encouragement. It is here that is kindled the ambition that makes a youngster yearn for appointment to the CID or the motor patrol, or any of the other specialist branches. The whole future stretches before them, full of enticing opportunities, the prospect of promotion, perhaps a chance to be groomed for the top at the Police College. There is idealism, too, the feeling of belonging to a useful service and doing a real job of work. For some, the years that follow will see early hopes fulfilled, for others, disappointment and disenchantment will set in. Yet nearly all policemen look back with some nostalgia to their early service and recall their first real incidents vividly, the thrill of the first arrest, the horror of the first fatal accident, the first clash with a bullying sergeant, and all kinds of similar happenings.

'I joined with a batch of lads from the army soon after the war,' a superintendent said. 'Most of them have gone long ago but there are some left, including one or two constables. I like to think that we are all still friends, because they are my contemporaries. I was one of the lucky ones, but as a young policeman you get this sense of belonging to the group that you joined with, and it stays with you right through your service, no matter what your rank is.'

4 Family

In 1970, a village shopkeeper banned a policeman's wife from his premises because her husband had reported him for a motoring offence. She had to go several miles to the nearest town for her groceries. The shopkeeper was within his rights; if he wished to be vindictive towards the policeman's family as a way of getting his own back, there was no law to stop him. For the unfortunate and embarrassed wife, the incident would be just another reminder of her special place. By marrying a policeman, a woman acquires something more than a husband. She becomes, whether she likes it or not, a part of the force. She must learn to accept her status and adapt her domestic routine to the constant requirements of the job, or persuade her husband, as so many wives do, to leave.

The policeman's wife is not alone in finding that her husband's occupation has a major influence on family life. A sailor's wife expects to be on her own for long periods, a soldier's wife expects either to be separated or to have to travel, wives of professional men are expected to make some contribution to their husband's careers. A police wife, however, can say, 'Me too' when any one of the things expected of other wives is mentioned. This is particularly true of the village constable's wife. 'I sometimes think I know more about the job than he does,' said a Kent police wife. 'Everyone seems to wait until they are sure he will be out before they start calling or ringing up. If we go out for the evening, which is once in a blue moon, he has to ring the divisional headquarters to let them know. They like to think that we keep a round-the-clock watch here.'

The rest of the policeman's family is not immune from the pressures of having a member of the force for a father. The survey on man-management reported that one in four of the policemen interviewed felt that their children had been bullied at school at some time because they were policeman's children. If a member of a police family appears in court, the newspaper headlines will say, 'PC's wife stole,' or, 'Police inspector's son on car charge.' The image of shining police integrity is expected to extend to all members of a policeman's family.

Although the time has passed when a policeman could not marry without permission, and then only after the authorities had approved his wife, police wives are still a long way short of becoming completely detached from their husband's obligations. The police regulations contain a rule which says that a policeman may be disqualified from his appointment if his wife, or any member of his family living with him, has an interest in licensed premises in the force area. There is also a rule which would disqualify a policeman if any member of his family had a business interest in the force area. The purpose of these regulations is to prevent any possible conflict of interest arising for a policeman, and to guarantee· his impartiality, but quite often the literal interpretation of the rules has caused difficulties and resentment. A widely reported recent case involving the rule about business interest concerned a policeman whose wife ran a theatrical agency. It was alleged that the policeman was involved in the business and he was obliged to resign following disciplinary proceedings. He said that other members of the force were jealous of his affluent way of life. This may have been true, but the force insists that a member must give his whole time to the service, and few forces would tolerate a situation in which a policeman's interests outside the job appeared to be taking up more time than he was spending on police work. Against this, the regulation is sometimes enforced in what appear to be quite trivial cases. 'My wife's aunties left her a stall in the market,' said a former Lancashire policeman. 'I asked the chief if she could go on running it and he refused. She'd worked there part-time for years and there was no objection to that, but now she was working for herself it was all wrong. The stall brought in less money than I got as a policeman, so we had to sell out for a lot less than it was worth.'

Sometimes, also, senior officers try to interfere when they disapprove of the type of job which a policeman's wife has taken. A constable whose wife worked as a clerk in a betting shop said, 'He told me it wasn't the kind of work a policeman's wife should be doing. I said that it was a properly run shop and there were no complaints about the place or he would have closed it. Know what he said? 'It's up to policemen and their families to give a lead against gambling, not to support it.' I had to tell her to pack it in because we'd have been transferred and with a girl at grammar school taking her O-levels it would have been awkward, you see.'

The police service lays so much emphasis upon contact with the public that involvement in community affairs would, one might think, be welcomed. Yet as recently as 1970 a Scottish chief inspector was threatened with disciplinary action unless his wife withdrew from a local council election. It took an approach to the Secretary of State for Scotland to secure a ruling that a policeman's wife was not debarred from politics, but there are many senior officers who would frown on the idea of a policeman's wife becoming a local councillor because it could be said to be endangering the traditional political impartiality of the force.

Regulations apart, there are other restrictions which face a policeman's family in their everyday lives. These are never defined in writing, but their implications are fully understood. A year or two ago a sergeant in a Welsh force and a constable were enjoying an evening out with their wives in a local pub when a superintendent paid an official call on the premises. The next morning the superintendent told the sergeant that he did not expect his men to frequent licensed premises in the division. The sergeant thought this was going too far, and complained to the local branch of the Police Federation. The chief constable's answer was that the sergeant had not been given an order, only a little wise advice. Soon afterwards, the sergeant was transferred some distance away to a predominantly Welsh-speaking area, although he and his family were not bilingual.

Much has been said and written of the village constable's impact upon a rural community, but for many police families there is a feeling of insecurity caused by the knowledge that their residence in any one place is temporary, liable to be changed by the whims of authority at any time and often at short notice.

Until very recently, county police forces in many parts of the country operated a policy on transfers which aimed at ensuring that no man spent more than three or four years in one place. The thinking which lay behind such a policy was that if a man spent too long at one station, he would lose his edge, become too friendly with the locals, and law enforcement would suffer. It was far from uncommon for newly appointed chief constables to embark upon wholesale transfers as soon as they took office. In a way, the policy was a tribute to the facility of country policemen for making friends with people, but to the official mind this very friendship was synonymous with idleness and even corruption. It was an echo of those days when, in 1971, the newspapers took up the story of a jovial Kent constable who, after sixteen years in one small village, was going to be moved even though he was due for retirement. It was said (but denied) that the transfer was a form of punishment because the constable did not report enough offenders. For days afterwards, the press carried features about the PC and his methods of keeping order, plus his admirably happy relations with the villagers. Nowadays, county forces have a more enlightened approach to the whole question of transfers, mainly because they too have their manpower problems. The human problems involved in a transfer are considerable: the complete removal of a family; the separation from neighbours and friends; school changes; family employment; a new home; and quite often a different environment. A Lancashire sergeant who moved on promotion from a country beat near the Westmorland border to a grimy South Lancashire town told me, 'It took us all a year to get used to it. My wife was miserable and the kids were unhappy. Even now it's only tolerable and we hust hope that the next move will take us back up there.'

A chief constable of the old school would be surprised to see the lengths to which many present-day chief officers will go to make sure that a transfer is in the best interests of the policeman concerned. They pay special attention to family matters, especially where children at school are likely to be affected. This approach ought to be universal in the service. Unfortunately, there are still some forces where it is not. 'My children had three moves in five years,' said a West Country constable. 'What chance have they got with the 11-plus or the GCE if they are always shunting around the county?' This man's wife was upset because her daughter had been moved from an excellent junior school in a town to a one-class village school with two teachers.

Quite recently, one inspector in a county force resigned several years short of his pension rather than obey an order to move to the opposite end of the county. He had pleaded with the chief constable to be allowed to stay in his present station until his daughter had taken her GCE a few months later. This was refused, the chief suggesting that the girl could live as a lodger with the inspector who was taking his place.

Some senior officers, whilst insisting that the wishes of the men are considered as far as possible, justify their attitude to transfers by saying that a man is aware, when he joins the force, that he can be required to move to any part of the force area. 'The real reason why a man doesn't want to be moved,' said a divisional superintendent, 'is often quite different from what he tells you. He'll say all kinds of things about the wife's health and the kid's education, but ten to one the real reason is that the wife has a nice little job. I know that's important to him, but what would the chief say if I said we couldn't move a policeman because of his wife's job?' This insistence on 'the job must come first' makes sense from the point of view of uncomplicated force administration, but a policeman's wife will have a different view. Police wives go out to work for the same economic motives as any other working wives, and there is bound to be resentment when the transfer of a policeman means the end of the family's second income. But there are other reasons which may make a policeman, especially an older man, reluctant to be transferred. 'Jobs don't grow on trees in this part of the world,' said a West Country constable. 'I can put my ticket in two years from now and get a job that will suit me nicely in the factory down the road. What I dread is being moved fifty miles away to some place at the back of beyond where there won't be any work when I finish in the force.'

The widespread amalgamations of the mid-sixties brought an important social change to many policemen. Before this, the county man had envied his colleague in the borough forces and the Metropolitan because they were allowed to become owner-occupiers, buying their homes with the aid of the generous 'rent' allowances whilst, in his case, the idea of buying his own home and putting permanent roots in one place was regarded as unthinkable. After the mergers, chief officers found that they had large numbers of owner-occupiers in their new forces, and in equity were forced to consider the claims of the old county force men to similar treatment.

Nowadays, all forces have some form of scheme for owner-occupiers, although there are usually limitations, such as restricting the right to buy a house to men with some years of service and specifying that there must not be too great a concentration of house-owners in one area. The question of house ownership by the police was one of the problems which the Home Office working party on management considered, and a report on the subject was published in 1970. It was, in many ways, a disappointing document because it left the general question of who could or could not become an owner-occupier to chief officers, and was unable to produce a practical scheme for financial assistance for house purchase. One stumbling block which faces chief constables who are modern enough to encourage home ownership by their men is the legacy of the house-building programmes carried out by the county forces after the war. Some forces have large stocks of police houses and most of the modern property is of a high standard. One solution would be to offer them for sale to their present occupants, but the market values are high and the Home Office has shown little enthusiasm for proposals to dispose of them in this way.

A chief constable who has made conscientious efforts to meet the wishes of his men to become owner-occupiers, and at the same time to face up to the operational requirements of his force, explained his problems to me. He said that he could not give absolute priority to a man's wishes, for the simple reason that operational needs could never be over-ruled by housing policies. His main operational responsibility was to have his largest concentration of personnel in the industrial belt in one part of his county. As it happened, this area was the least desirable from a residential standpoint and most of the applications to become owner-occupiers were in respect of areas where he had more than enough police already. 'What am I to do?' this chief constable asked. 'Transfer men out of the country districts and into the towns simply to make room for owner-occupiers? If I scrapped all restrictions I would have policemen where I did not need them and very few where I did.'

This chief constable shared with many of his colleagues in the top ranks the view that a policeman who wanted to own his own house might have to make a decision one day not to pursue his promotion ambitions. 'I believe,' he said, 'that a newly promoted officer has a better chance of becoming efficient in his new rank if he has new surroundings.' The theory is that an officer who has just assumed additional disciplinary responsibilities has an easier transition to authority if he is removed from the immediate company of his former comrades. County chief constables are unimpressed by the argument that this did not happen in the days of the small borough forces.

Again, for reasons of operational efficiency, chief constables do not like their men to live too far away from their place of duty The fact that married constables have motor cars does not weigh with them, yet in the Metropolitan Police many officers have journeys of more than ten miles in each direction.

One senior officer told me that the modern trend to encourage owner-occupation would prove to be a mistake. It was being done, he said, as a sop to prevent wastage, but it ran counter to all the thinking behind other developments such as unit beat policing and fewer and larger police forces. 'On the one hand we are saying that it is desirable that the man on the unit beat should live on his beat, on the other we are saying that he can buy his own house. What will happen is that you will have one unit beat with about two dozen policemen living on it, and no one living on a beat where the area is not so desirable.'

The strength of the owner-occupiers in the police force has risen in the past twenty years from a fairly insignificant number to a figure approaching half the total number of married men in the force. (About forty thousand police were buying their homes in 1970). The owner-occupier has a considerable financial advantage over his married colleague living in a rent-free police house. Originally, rent allowance was paid in lieu of a free house, so that the man who was not provided with police premises was not at a disadvantage. Now the pendulum has swung completely away. After spending his entire service in a police house, the occupant has nothing to show for it on retirement. The owner-occupier who reaches this status early in his service will have paid for his house before retirement, almost entirely from the rent allowance, which is tax free, and based on housing costs in the area. For some years, the authorities have wanted to end the system by consolidating rent allowance with pay. This would have an advantage for the authorities in presenting the true level of police pay in a much more favourable light, and for the man in enhancing the value of his police pension, but the idea is strongly resisted by the police. This opposition is because rent allowances, which are negotiated locally, have more than kept pace with spiralling housing costs, while consolidation would mean that the initial advantage to the man would rapidly evaporate in times of inflation.

After the war, when housing was in demand, there were waiting lists for police houses. While the standard of those built may have been good, there are often complaints from police families about their location. 'This is not a bad house from a building point of view,' said a constable in a city force, 'but the location is bloody terrible.' The house he lived in was one of a pair in the middle of a large council estate. 'Half the neighbours have got form,' said the constable, 'one or two of them you think of automatically by the CRO number, if you see what I mean. They are the last people in the world I would choose for neighbours. My kids go to the same school as their kids, and if I insist that they don't play with them, it makes it rough on them. We don't like living here, and most of them don't want us.'

There has been a tendency, mainly dictated by finance, to group police houses so that police families live in close proximity to each other. This was criticized by the Royal Commission as tending to emphasize the isolation between the police and the public, but it is often unpopular with the police themselves. 'It was a bit like living in army barracks,' said a constable who had moved out of police property to become an owner-occupier. 'Everyone around knew all your business. The wives were nosey and jealous and if one man got promoted it sometimes led to awkwardness.'

Policemen, understandably, get annoyed when, as so often happens, local residents object to police houses being sited close to their properties. 'You would think they would be bloody glad to have us,' said a London constable who lives in a police house in a select area, 'but the cheeky buggers went and asked for a reduction in their rates because they said that we were tenants. Some of them won't acknowledge you in the garden. They're mortgaged up to their necks but they like to pretend they are upper class.' Whatever policemen think of this kind of snobbery, it does not prevent the police owner-occupier from feeling that he has bettered himself in moving out of a police house. 'I became an owner-occupier to get away from a police house,' said another London constable. 'When I shut that front door behind me, that's it.'

Policemen, and to some extent their relatives, have to get used to many small examples of reserve which other people show in their presence. The policeman's wife, for instance, knows why she is sometimes served first in the village shop — a particularly juicy bit of village gossip is under discussion. 'The PTA was having a Christmas bazaar,' said one wife, 'and one of the committee mentioned we couldn't have a raffle if we sent tickets through the post because it wasn't legal. Someone else said it didn't matter and the chairman said, "We'll just pretend that Mrs Briggs didn't hear that, won't we?" and everyone laughed. I was blazing inside.'

Some people appear to take a rather smug delight in reminding policemen's families that they are expected to behave in an irreproachable fashion. 'My son got into a scrape at school,' said a London inspector. 'There were three others involved and it amounted to nothing more than horseplay. We got a letter from the headmaster saying that if there was a repetition he would have to suspend the boy. Fair enough. But when he said that this was not the kind of conduct he expected from a policeman's son, I wrote back to ask what my job had to do with it. I'm the policeman in the family, not him.'

In common with other parents, policemen know the domestic friction which can arise between growing youngsters and their fathers. Often, their attitude towards youthful behaviour is conditioned by their own views, as policemen,

on social matters. Equally, a policeman's adolescent children
are likely to resent a father who appears to be adopting
police attitudes in the home. It may be true that policemen
are anxious about their children because they dread the
embarrassment that would follow if a child of theirs got into
trouble with the law. The family influence can be counter-
acted by opposite pressures from school and other youngsters, where a policeman's son is afraid of becoming
something of an outsider in his own age group.

On the point about bullying at school, mentioned in the
management survey, a force welfare officer said, 'I have
known policemen ask for a transfer because of the hostile
attitude of other children at school. If the man works in an
area with a fairly high crime rate, it stands to reason that
some children will be affected by the anti-police attitude of
their parents, and try to take it out on a policeman's
children. It is rare, but it can happen.'

'Every father worries about his kids,' said a London
sergeant, 'and I've done my share. My eldest got in with a bad
lot at school and finished up on probation. I was shattered, I
can tell you. A policeman's son on probation. I still can't
understand it. I tried everything, but it seems that deep inside
he's got a deep dislike of me because I'm a policeman.' The
parents had spoken to a psychiatrist who had examined the
boy during his period on probation. 'He told my husband this
bit about John disliking the police and his father being in it.
But what is he supposed to do, give up his work because his
son doesn't like it? I think it's nonsense.'

It is perhaps inevitable that in some police families, the
children will resent attempts by parents to make them
conform to their own rigid standards of respectability,
especially if they suspect that what lies behind such attitudes
is a fear that their actions as policemen's children will reflect
on them. The village policeman, living in a police house, finds
it harder to keep his police life separate from his family than
either the owner-occupier in the borough or the metropolitan
policeman who lives some distance away from his work. 'The

neighbours round here know I'm a policeman,' said a London detective, 'but my station is ten miles away. Professionally, I don't come into contact with any of the people I live near. When I'm at home, I'm just plain Mister. Why should it be any different?' Detectives are more likely to find that the job creates pressures on their personal lives than the uniformed men, with their comparatively regular duties. 'The only time I can guarantee I will spend a lot of time with the family is on a long weekend or annual leave,' said a London detective inspector. 'Even with leave, you have to be very careful about trial dates. Once I had to cut short a holiday on the continent to give evidence in an adjourned case. You just have to get used to coming home to find the house in darkness with everyone asleep.'

Some promising younger detectives have applied to return to uniformed duty, not because they have lost their enthusiasm for CID work, but because of the strain on their marriages. A detective in a southern county force asked to be put on permanent office duty, knowing that it would stop his promotion chances, because of trouble at home. 'Our son got into trouble with a right crowd of young tearaways,' he said,'I was too busy to take much notice until one night there was a call from another nick to say that he and another lad had been picked up for taking and driving away a car. It was like being kicked in the stomach, I can tell you. Of course, I wanted to have it out with him as soon as we got home, but the wife went for me. When was I ever at home, she wanted to know. What interest did I take in the kids? It was work, work, work, all the time. Well, I realized it had to stop. I've got two younger children, and I don't want them going the same way.'

Where children are involved, a policeman's wife often finds that she has not only to assume the major share of looking after them, because the father on shift work is out of the house so much during evenings and weekends, but she also has to avoid disturbing his rest during the daytime. 'When my two were very young they must have thought I had an ogre upstairs,' said a Yorkshire wife. 'I was always on at them to be quiet. He's a light sleeper and we used to have rows if he woke up.'

The influence of a wife on a policeman's career is hard to define. If her husband is ambitious, she has to accept that his pursuit of promotion will involve a certain number of sacrifices in the home. 'We used to keep the telly off when he was studying,' said an inspector's wife. 'I used to sit with Moriarty's *Police Law* while he learned definitions and Acts of Parliament off by heart. The tension really built up as the exam got nearer.'

'When my husband qualified for the Police College,' said a Birmingham wife, 'I suddenly realised that he was going to be away for a year and our first baby was on the way. I felt at the time that he was not being fair, that promotion wasn't worth that. Now it's behind us, but it still seems wrong to me.'

'The ultra-ambitious copper has to be a bit cold-blooded about his family,' said a young senior officer. 'My wife has had to put up with a lot. I realized we would have to move around a bit if I was going to get on, and it has meant giving up a lot. When I was young it was studying for exams. Then I was away at the college and on detective courses. Then it was moving from one force to another as I went up the ladder. She just had to tag along, doing all the moving and settling the kids down in a succession of houses. We both happen to think it's all been worth it, but don't underestimate what is involved. If a policeman wants to get to the top, his wife must want the same thing for him.'

There is a type of police wife whose determination that her husband shall succeed can lead to embarrassing problems for the man. 'The chief's wife used to come to weekly whist drives in the police club when we were a small force,' said an ex-borough sergeant. 'All the wives whose husbands were bobbing for promotion used to go. We used to argue about whether more promotions were decided at the whist drive than the Masonic Lodge.'

Wives who feel bitter because their husbands appear to have been passed over for promotion have been known to protest to senior officers, and promotion rivalry between wives has caused trouble amoung neighbouring police families. 'We got on really well with our next door neighbours until my husband was made sergeant,' said a Yorkshire wife. 'Because hers was still a constable she started being funny and made some nasty remarks about me in the shops. There was a row and it finished up with us being transferred just to get away from her.'

Many policemen will insist that their wives stay aloof from police affairs. They suspect that police social clubs are used by some wives as a means of currying favour with senior officers. 'I never go in the police club when I'm off duty,' said a Midlands constable. 'If I'm having a night out, I don't want to be in a police station with a lot of other police. I want a change, and so does my wife.'

Against this attitude, there are many police wives who enjoy social activities within the force. 'We've got a police wives group at the station,' said an inspector's wife. 'It's like any other women's club but we started it because we wanted something different from WIs or Townswomen's Guilds. We help with the children's party at Christmas and things like that but we never discuss police matters. The thing is, we've all got this one thing in common, our husbands are policemen. We're all friends. What's wrong with that?'

The remarkable success of the International Police Association is some indication that many policemen, whatever the attitude of others, do not want to shun each other socially. Started after the war by a Lincolnshire sergeant, the IPA now has thriving branches throughout the world, and organizes hundreds of holiday exchanges between police families in various countries. 'It is not just a cheap way of getting a holiday abroad,' said an IPA member. 'We do it because we are really proud of being what we are, and we've found that foreign policemen feel just the same way about the job.'

For a service with such a pride in its traditions, the police do not have the strong family associations which might be expected. There are, of course, many examples of police families which can trace their membership back to the early days of policing, but such cases seem to be fewer among the present-day force. 'I don't want my son to join just because I was in,' said a senior officer. 'A few years ago, I would have tried to stop him if he'd wanted to. Now that career prospects are so much better, I wouldn't mind him following me in the job, but I don't think he will. He's seen too much of the drawbacks.'

As more and more police families acquire their own homes (and as police forces become larger and more impersonal) the probability is that they will become less obviously 'different' from their neighbours. The village policemen, themselves a rapidly dwindling group, may be succeeded in the public eye by the modern 'neighbourhood' or 'unit beat' constables. Here, because of the support services provided by police stations, radios and cars, it is unlikely that the police wife will have to assume the old village PC's wife's role of the unpaid additional arm of the law.

'I don't look any different from anyone else,' said a Kent wife, 'I don't feel different, and I don't want to be different.'

5 Training

It is obvious, when the complex nature of a policeman's duties is considered, that proper training is essential. The service has a comprehensive training programme for recruits and probationers based on a network of district training centres staffed by police instructors, while the Metropolitan Police trains its own recruits at Hendon. The Police College at Bramshill House in Hampshire trains promising young sergeants and inspectors to be the senior officers of the near future and provides courses in top level administration for chief officers.

Apart from the promising but still limited scheme by which young Bramshill-trained sergeants and inspectors take degree courses at universities, police training is wholly internal. British policemen tend to scoff when they hear of American universities which give degrees in police sciences, or read of the many 'colleges' in the USA where potential police recruits take diploma courses before they are accepted into a force.

The service has always had a strong distrust of anything which seems remotely academic or intellectual. Between the wars, when Lord Trenchard was endeavouring to introduce a better type of senior officer into the Metropolitan Police by recruiting former public schoolboys and graduates for the Metropolitan Police College, the entire service was outraged by what it regarded as a violation of Peel's basic principle that the police should provide their own commanders. In fact, the Metropolitan and most provincial forces had always brought in its top commanders from outside, usually from the armed forces, but Trenchard appeared to be challenging a century-old tradition that promotion in the service was based on steady and unspectacular progress from the bottom of the ladder. Indeed, just about the most wounding thing which one policeman can say about another is that he is 'just a book policeman', implying that the qualities which a policeman prizes above most others, common sense and practical ability, are completely lacking.

'There isn't a university in the world which can teach a copper how to feel a collar,' said a senior CID man, expressing a viewpoint which would be endorsed by the great majority of experienced officers. The CID is one department of the force where serious criticism of the specialist training given by the two detective training schools at Wakefield and Hendon is rarely made. This may be due to the fact that both are staffed by experienced practical detectives and the courses are heavily weighted on the side of practice rather than theory. The same can be said of the other large scale specialist training scheme for police drivers.

Each year, the recruit training centres provide a three months' initial course for between five and six thousand recruits. About a quarter of the students are former police cadets and as such they will have a rudimentary knowledge of the subjects taught before they go to the training centre. The remainder will be men and women between nineteen and thirty years of age with different backgrounds and varying intelligence, all taking a course which is frankly admitted to be strictly elementary and geared to the average level. One discouraging feature is that the staffs of the centres work in the knowledge that almost half of the students will have left the police within two or three years of joining.

Each centre takes recruits from every force in its area. They are taught subjects which are common to police work everywhere and the separate forces must supplement this basic training with local procedure courses when the students return to their forces. Each new intake provides the instructors with an illuminating insight into the recruiting problems of each force. 'Some forces in this region are nearly up to strength,' said one instructor, 'so they are able to pick and choose a bit. We have one large city force which is one of the most undermanned in the country. Naturally, a lot of their recruits are pretty poor material and we do the best we can, but some are hopeless. You know it's a waste of your time because they are not going to stay, or they will never amount to much as policemen.'

Recruits go to the centres as soon as they are appointed as constables, receiving full basic pay and free accommodation while in training. The training syllabus is designed to teach a recruit the essentials of his job in a very short period. The course devotes a third of the available time to police law, ranging from general statutes to serious crimes. Road traffic instruction takes up about a sixth of the course, and the remainder is spent on drilling, swimming, first aid and self-defence. That there are deficiencies in the basic course is acknowledged by the fact that for some time now a comprehensive review of police training has been in progress. The course has evolved rather than been planned and has remained relatively unaltered since the district training centres were opened after the war to cope with an anti-cipated influx of recruits. The administration of the centres, and therefore the contents of the syllabus, has been the exclusive concern of the chief constables in each area. They have not reacted kindly to criticism of the centres and have resisted attempts by the Police Federation to secure a foothold in the management committees.

One of the most persistent problems affecting the training centres has been a dearth of able instructors. As they are exclusively police officers, they have to be detached from their own forces. Unless an instructor is able to move his family with him, his work involves separation from his home for five days a week. Again, instructors are reluctant to spend more than a year or two at training centres because all promotion is based upon their own force and they fear that a lengthy spell of detachment will take them out of the running.

While under training, the police recruit lives a life which can be regarded as wholly artificial compared with what is in store for him when he returns. When on the beat, he will be expected to act on his own initiative, whereas he trains alongside thirty other recruits and is under constant supervision from the centre staff. Discipline is perhaps more rigorous than he will find it in his force. As well as the ordinary rules of conduct designed to ensure smooth operation of the centre and the comfort of other residents, he will learn to respond to words of command on the parade ground

'We are the first people to take a good look at a recruit,' said another instructor. 'All the force knows about him is what they've got on paper and the impression they've got from interviews. We see him as a person, how he reacts to training, how he gets on with other people, what kind of a man he is. It all goes into a report when he rejoins his force, but I often wonder if anyone takes any notice. More than once I've said that a man was obviously unsuitable, but he's been kept on in the force. I suppose the chief constable thinks he knows better than we do.'

A singular lack of imagination has characterized recruit-training in the police service. The initial course is wholly concentrated upon purely police subjects. Recruits are expected to digest large slabs of legislation in order to pass the various course examinations. In the process, the brighter ones manage to absorb a vast amount of knowledge which, for the most part, is virtually useless to them as they begin their careers as beat constables. It is hard to understand why recruits should be taught the law on all manner of serious and even obscure crimes when the chances of having to deal with any of them in their first years as policemen are very remote. For the recruit who is not intellectually equipped for such a course, the training centre can only serve to convince him that he has taken on a job that is beyond his capabilities and herein lies a probable explanation for many of the very early resignations.

I believe that the service misses a good opportunity to

make much better use of a recruit's first period. (Most recruits return to the centres for refresher courses at the end of their probation.) If the course could be radically altered so that far less time was spent upon the accumulation of legal knowledge of dubious worth and more upon introducing the recruit to the police service and its role in the community, the centres might begin to play a much more significant part in the general training field. The present course teaches a recruit almost nothing about the way in which the service has evolved; the relationship between its members and the general public; the social problems which policemen encounter every day of their working lives; the function of supervisory officers and leadership in the forces; the degree of discretion open to a police officer in the prosecution of offences (all recruit training assumes that the offence will be followed by a charge). The service has been so slow to make even modest adjustments to its recruit-training programme that only recently have the centres included one short lecture on race relations.

If training centres spent less time on purely legal matters, some part of the course could be used to give instructors an opportunity to study the individual student in some depth. Nothing is known of a recruit on his arrival and he is practically an unknown quantity to the force which has appointed him. A course which included greater opportunities to participate in discussions and projects designed to test initiative and attitudes, and took note of social factors in society, would be bound to reveal more of the man inside the uniform that the present course can hope to discover. If, for this purpose, the instructors included educationalists and other non-police personnel, the picture to emerge would be more reliable. The police instructor would be able to assess the individual's potential as a policeman, which is of primary importance, but an educationalist or a psychiatrist might be able to tell a chief officer something about the student as a human being.

Writing in advance of the conclusions of the current review

of training, I doubt if they will follow this line at all. The control of recruit-training is secure in the hands of chief constables and, to a lesser extent, the Home Office. The local authorities keep their usual parsimonious grip on the financial side. The chief constables, because of their manpower problems, are anxious to get their recruits back from the centres as soon as possible. The local authorities, well aware of the high cost of training, are unlikely to be interested in proposals which might appear to be mere frills. I believe that a major reconstruction of the initial training courses would not only be of more lasting use to the student and his force, but would help to reduce premature wastage. In the long run, this would lead to a saving of expenditure on training or at least ensure that the money was being spent in a better cause.

The present initial training course appears to be based on the principle that no recruit can be let loose on the public without a proper understanding of his duties, responsibilities and powers. This is quite true, of course, but it is very doubtful if the course achieves its objective. 'We might as well tell them to forget everything they have learned at the training centre,' a superintendent in a northern force told me. 'Three quarters of it is superfluous, stuff they will never have to deal with. The truth is that most policemen learn by experience and being taught by others. A good patrol sergeant will teach a recruit more than a training centre ever could.'

All police probationers spend the greater part of their first two years engaged in some form of training. After the initial course, there are local procedure classes and some of the more advanced forces have their own residential courses for local instruction. During his probation the recruit will spend long periods on attachment to the various specialist departments of the force for the purpose of gaining an insight into the broader structure of its organization. While on probation, he will be subject to close supervision by sergeants and inspectors who are expected to help him with any incidents he has to deal with on the beat. This is the way in which the recruit has the opportunity to learn his job, no simulated classroom exercise can teach him more about a case of petty theft than his first arrest. Perhaps in the process be begins to appreciate the irrelevance of much of his initial training course. In their detailed study of police manpower,* Martin and Wilson comment, 'If full use is to be made of the capital that is being invested in the service all ranks will have to be trained to understand the implications of mobility and communications. It may well be that the police officer will need to know less about law, for advice will be easier to come by, but more about the tactics of operations.' A start could and should be made in this direction at the outset of a policeman's career by including in the initial course a broad introduction to modern police organization and working methods, particularly the implications of unit beat policing, improved accumulation of information and use of criminal intelligence (in other words, showing a recruit how to keep his eyes and ears open on his beat); and to be really up to date the course could include the work of the national police computer.

Martin and Wilson, however, appear to be taking the training process much further than the initial stages. That there is a need for more training throughout the service and at all levels would be evident to any outside consultants making a survey of police organization and efficiency. Between the recruit training scheme and the Police College higher training courses exists a huge void which is hardly touched by the local courses which a few forces provide for experienced constables and newly promoted sergeants and inspectors, and certainly not by the pre-examination 'cramming courses' for promotion candidates. In the past twenty years, new legislation has been issuing from Westminster at a rapidly accelerating rate. Some of it has been fairly inconsequential, bringing existing statutes up to date, but much of it has been fundamental, such as the Theft

*J.P. Martin and Gail Wilson, *The Police, a Study in Manpower* (London, 1967)

Act which superseded most of the previous law. The trend towards an eventual codified criminal law is inexorable. Yet many police officers are left virtually to their own devices and have to rely upon Home Office circulars to keep themselves up to date. Understandably, many policemen do not make the effort to keep abreast of changes when little or no assistance is provided. While the value of teaching criminal law to raw recruits is slight, the need to keep experienced operational officers in touch with changes is important.

It is the policeman who is attempting to pass the promotion examinations who is most concerned with keeping abreast of legal changes. The remainder, who constitute a majority, have less incentive to do so. Police regulations decree that a policeman who wishes to be promoted from constable to sergeant or from sergeant to inspector must have obtained a pass in the appropriate examination. (Advancement to the higher ranks is by selection without examination.) Until the mid-sixties, the examinations were in two parts, educational and professional. The educational papers were dropped after it was realized that the professional examinations were in themselves a fairly stiff test of a candidate's academic standard. They call for an intelligent understanding of criminal and traffic law, and of general police duties. A successful candidate must be able to write lucid and comprehensive replies. It is not over-stating the case to say that the standard of police examinations is at least as high as those for law students in the same subjects.

When one compares the low standard of police entrance examinations with the advanced knowledge of law required to pass the promotion examination, the anomaly is obvious. Many police recruits are accepted who cannot hope to reach promotion standard because of the examination, and some must become discouraged and resign when they realize this. In all forces it is possible to find men who are regarded as excellent policemen, some of them skilful and valuable detectives, to whom promotion is an impossible dream. The Metropolitan Police, which has maintained its own system of competitive examinations ever since the war ended, makes some concession to this human problem by reserving a small percentage of sergeants' vacancies for men who have managed to pass the examination, but not with high enough marks to qualify for automatic promotion under the competitive system.

The standard promotion examination for all provincial forces in England and Wales was introduced in the fifties, largely in response to complaints by the Police Federation about the wide variation in local examinations. The papers set in most forces before this were hardly a promotion obstacle. Most chief constables were unimpressed by professional knowledge and the local tests were kept as elementary as possible. The regulations stated that a man must have passed an appropriate examination before being promoted, but chief constables wanted to be free to select their men from as wide a field as possible. Naturally, such a system was wide open to accusations of favouritism. But the first results of the standard examination were a rude shock for the police. Only about a fifth of the candidates passed. In some forces, notably the heavily undermanned ones, the pass rate was less than ten per cent. Some chief constables were faced with a situation in which there were more promotion vacancies than there were qualified men to fill them.

The high failure rate was due to a combination of factors. In a sense, they confirmed the view of many that the standard of police recruiting had declined alarmingly. It was not a coincidence that the question of the ability of the police to provide their future leaders themselves began to be discussed at about the same time as the depressing first results of the standard examination became known. Some chief constables, on the other hand, described the standard set by the examiners as ridiculous. Candidates had to pass five separate papers in one sitting and the set questions were criticized as being too obscure and academic.

Over the years, the pass rate has improved until nowadays about half the ten thousand candidates who sit the examination each year manage to qualify. There have been major changes which have helped to achieve this. The number of papers has been reduced from five to three, and an aggregate pass mark has been introduced, so that a candidate could fail one paper (or even two) and still secure enough marks overall to pass. Just as significant has been the change which allows constables to sit the examination after completing two years' service, while their training is still fresh in their minds, rather than having to wait for at least four years. More important still, every force now has a local training scheme.

The only immediate reward for passing the promotion examination is a once-for-all payment of thirty pounds, recommended in 1962 by the Royal Commission on the Police as an incentive. The improved pass rate means that, in all forces except the Metropolitan, promotion is by selection from among those qualified. There is a complete divergence of view between the provinces and the Metropolitan on the examination question. The Metropolitan bases its examination on its own instruction book. Its competitive system covers all promotion up to the rank of inspector. A successful candidate knows, by his examination mark, where he stands in the promotion queue. Although in theory a member cannot sit the competitive examination without a certificate of fitness for promotion signed by his superintendent, it is extremely rare for this to be witheld. The competitive system is extremely popular with the force, who would fight just as hard to keep it as the provincial police will fight to resist it being extended to their forces. A recent attempt by the Police Federation's national executive to convince the membership of the merits of the competitive system met with an overwhelming defeat at the national conference. In this, the delegates were expressing the policeman's traditional distrust of scholarship, even in professional subjects. 'I don't see why the examination should be the only factor in promotion,' said a force training officer. 'At best it is no more than a guide to what a policeman knows about law. It doesn't tell a thing about him as a man. No examination can test a man as a leader.'

The police promotion examinations play a dual role in the training and promotion side of police affairs. Apart from assessing candidates for promotion to sergeant and inspector, they are also the first stage in the selection process which takes promising young constables to the Police College and a place on the 'Special' Course, designed to groom them for senior rank in fairly quick time. In many ways, the Special Course is the most significant development to have taken place in the internal organization of the police service since the war.

The Police College opened its doors a few years after the war to provide some form of higher training for sergeants who were expected to become inspectors, and for superintendents who were close to becoming chief officers. This was the first institution to operate on a national basis. Trenchard's short-lived Hendon Police College was an exclusively Metropolitan affair, introduced after the economic crises of the early thirties had killed an earlier scheme for a national college. The objectives of Hendon, as envisaged by Trenchard, and of the post-war Police College were different in one vital aspect. Trenchard wanted to attract well-educated outsiders who were interested in a career as a senior police officer, as well as to provide advanced training for promising material already in the force. The Police College was only concerned with the training of serving policemen.

From its inception, and largely because of the unhappy recollections of Trenchard's ideas, the college has been expected to conform to the police commitment to the twin principles of promotion from within and equality of opportunity. In its early years, this commitment was so total as to nullify almost any prospect of the college making a major contribution to police training or influencing the selection of senior officers. By the end of the fifties, however, those close enough to the college to see what was happening were well aware of its failure to make much impact on police affairs. The main difficulty was that the college had no say in the choice of students, most of whom (in the case of sergeants) were too old to gain any lasting benefit from a six months' course divided between professional studies and a sketchy introduction to the liberal arts. Chief constables who distrusted such innovations showed their contempt for the college by deliberately nominating sergeants whom they had no intention of promoting. In any case, the strictly limited accommodation meant that only a handful of the inspectors promoted each year would have been on a course. The fact that the first two Commandants were both senior army officers was unpopular with with many policemen, including senior officers, and contributed to the suspicion which surrounded the college in its first years.

Also near the end of the fifties came a series of incidents involving chief constables and senior officers of provincial forces. One was sent to prison for embezzlement, another was severely criticized for the chaotic state of discipline in his force, and a third was acquitted in the notorious Brighton conspiracy trial in which two of his subordinates were gaoled and the judge commented upon the poor quality of leadership in the force. As it happened, the chief constables in the country could be divided roughly into two groups at that time, those who had 'come up the hard way' from the ranks, and the elite corps of ex-Hendon men in command of most of the larger forces and very much in evidence in the Scotland Yard hierarchy. Well-informed commentators on police affairs began to speculate about the future once the Hendon-trained commanders departed.

Perhaps it was anxiety on this point which prompted the Home Office to institute an inquiry into higher training for the police. From this emerged, mainly at the instigation of the then senior Inspector of Constabulary, Sir William Johnson, the plans for the Special Course. These were based upon a general acknowledgement of the need of the service to identify its potential leaders early in their careers. Only the Metropolitan Police and the largest provincial forces offered even a medium-term prospect of promotion to the highest posts for able officers. Elsewhere, seniority was the main consideration. It was recognized that most of the men who were going to the college at that time were well advanced in service as well as age. The Johnson plan, which introduced the Special Course, was aimed at the bright young constable. If he could be found soon enough, given a longer and more sophisticated course designed to develop his powers of leadership, and sent back to his force as a young sergeant who could expect quick promotion to inspector, there would be a nucleus of able young men ready to assume greater responsibilities in the near future.

It was a modest scheme by comparison with the standards of the armed forces, the civil service, and industry, but it was revolutionary for the police. Even then, it almost foundered because of the well-meaning but misguided insistence of the police themselves, and especially the Police Federation, to subordinate every other consideration to the sacred cow of fairness of opportunity. In this case, fairness was supposed to be ensured by giving the twelve men who had secured the highest marks in the year's promotion examination an automatic place on the first Special Course, and selecting the remainder, by an extended interview process, from among those who had come slightly lower in the list. The Metropolitan Police, not involved in the provincial examination, were allocated a quota of places on the course, although their own commanders doubted if their men would gain any benefit from it.

One year's experience of this system convinced all parties that no man should have a prescriptive right to a Special Course place, and from then on the selection procedures have been widened to the point where any young man who has passed the examination will be considered. But for several years the selection field was restricted to the few hundred men who had scored the highest marks in the examination. It was this that encouraged chief constables to develop their force training programme for examination candidates, some of which were unashamed 'cramming' courses reserved for the bright young officers with the best chance of securing a place at the college.

Another important lesson learned from the early years of the scheme was that only young men could derive real benefit from the course and have any real prospect of justifying the scheme by advancing to senior rank at an early age. The Special Course is now almost exclusively made up of young constables (under thirty) with less than ten years' service, and preferably much less. They are selected after a paper sift of all examination passes and an interview with a regional selection board, which passes on recommended candidates to the final selectors at the extended interviews. Those chosen go to the college as sergeants and, after completing the course successfully, they return to their own force and are automatically promoted to inspector after another year. The original idea was that there would be no automatic promotion beyond sergeant and successful college students would still have to pass the examination to inspector and wait to be promoted in the normal way. In practice, this meant that very few men were getting the accelerated promotion considered necessary. And so, in spite of the determined opposition of the Police Federation, these changes were brought in.

The Special Course has had some success in that a few of its graduates have become superintendents before they reached their thirtieth birthdays, and each year at least a dozen students go on to universities where some good degrees have been obtained in law and other subjects. On the debit side, it is a fact that only once has the course reached its full quota of sixty students and mostly the number has been around the forty mark. It is claimed that the figure of sixty really relates only to accommodation at the college, but it is evident that, of the five or six thousand men who pass the examination each year, about two-thirds of whom would qualify on age grounds, only about forty are considered to be of the potential to rise to senior rank in a reasonably short time.

In these circumstances, it is not surprising that there has been a long standing argument within the service about the methods of selection. On the figures of acceptances for the Special Course, it appears that the police force, whatever its other excellent qualities, is very short of potential leaders. The selectors insist that to fill up each year's course would be to debase its standard. Their critics argue that, on the contrary, an artificially high standard has been set and that it would be better to take a chance on a few more borderline cases in the hope that they will benefit from the course. It is alleged that the selectors will only send to Bramshill young constables whom they regard as cast-iron certainties for the top. Only a comparative handful of their choices fail to secure certificates of successful completion of the course. As one of the selectors himself admitted, 'As I see it, once a man gets on the course he is likely to stay there and, short of throwing cabbage at the Commandant on Mess Night, he will get his certificate.'

While the Special Course, and indeed all the activities of the Police College, are part of the general scheme of police training, albeit for a favoured and presumably talented few, it is significant that a study of all the papers, meetings and official correspondence dealing with the course are dominated by arguments over the selection procedure and contain precious little references to the course syllabus or, for that matter, its objectives as a programme of further education in professional and general studies. It is impossible to escape the conclusion that the authorities are more concerned with identifying future leaders and getting them into the Bramshill-university hothouse in the hope that they will emerge as soon as possible as ideal commanders, than they are anxious to ensure that their training is relevant to their future responsibilities.

Housed in a superb Jacobean mansion, Bramshill House, near Hartley Wintney in Hampshire, the college is the police service's academic shop-window. It has changed considerably from its early intentions, so much so that most inspectors are now given their short course in higher training at a new annexe to the college housed in a former RAF station in Yorkshire, while Bramshill concentrates on its fledgeling top brass and its courses for intermediate and senior commanders.

When the police recruiting advertisements speak of sergeants with three years' service and inspectors with five, they mean the Special Course men. What Bramshill has now established, in spite of the entrenched conservatism of the police themselves, it a clearly defined and deliberate avenue of unimpeded progress to the top. After the Special Course and university, a dynamic young inspector will not be with his force long before returning to the college for the Intermediate Command Course and then, in his mid-thirties or thereabouts, he should put the finishing touches to his preparation for top ranking at the Senior Command Course. The irony of the whole arrangement is that, taking out the element of public school and university entry at inspector level, Bramshill has quietly created precisely the structure which Trenchard wanted to secure with his Hendon scheme.

What Bramshill has not succeeded in doing (and, for that matter, it may not be trying to) is to find universal acceptance in the service. It is still looked upon with either condescension or suspicion by many policemen who will never be its students. The Special Course man returning to his force after a year at the college or a longer absence at university knows that he has to find acceptance on his own level, from subordinates and equals who will resent his advantages and implied certainty of further advancement. One notes that one of the main features of college life is its regular guest nights with distinguished visitors. Surprisingly, it seems, Bramshill has never extended an invitation to the service at large to see for themselves what goes on at the college. In the circumstances, they can hardly complain if the general weight of uniformed service opinion about the work of the directing staff is rather less than complimentary.

Bramshill's success or failure, both as a seat of advanced training for the police and as a provider of leaders, is yet to come. When the last survivors of pre-war Hendon have retired from the top posts, they will be succeeded for the most part by college-trained officers. It is on the general quality of their leadership that a final judgement on Bramshill can be made. It will be a judgement on the value of that bed-rock principle that the police must find their own commanders. One wonders whether the chief constables and senior officers of the future will be able to compensate for the lack of experience of ordinary police duty which must be the price of so many lengthy periods spent in the idyllic surroundings of Bramshill or the years at university.

Perhaps the problem is not as great as this. The role of senior administrators in the police service is changing with the service, and in many ways it is the quality of junior and middle-ranking leaders which is going to be more important than the lead set from the top. Here the danger is that the service has been concentrating too much upon establishing Bramshill on a level with the Sandhursts and the Cranwells and paying too little attention to the wider training requirements of experienced constables and sergeants.

Meanwhile, Bramshill is by far the most interesting and advanced part of the training arrangements. Only the Metropolitan's cadet scheme can match it in scope and attainment. If, in some future radical overhaul of training involving recruits, serving constables and sergeants, inspectors and the 'high-flyers' destined for the top, Bramshill became something less than a quasi-university and more of a central base for all police instruction, with a general responsibility for the regional establishments, a pattern more suited to the needs of the modern police would emerge.

6 Promotion and leadership

To adopt a famous army recruiting slogan, every young policeman carries a chief constable's baton in his truncheon pocket. Indeed, the phrase is much more accurate than the old *canard* about field marshals, for the service has nothing to compare with the military in the way of direct entry to officer rank. Every recruit, at least in theory and regulation, starts off on the same footing.

A study of the career biographies of the seventy men who fill the chief officers' posts today, however, would reveal a different picture. Well above half of them began in the Metropolitan Police under either Lord Trenchard or his successor, Sir Philip Game. They are products of public schools and universities, who joined the force in order to be trained, after a few months on the beat, at Trenchard's Metropolitan Police College at Hendon. From here they were gazetted to the now defunct rank of junior station inspector, young men intended to reach senior rank while in their thirties.

Mention of Trenchard and Hendon, even today, is still enough to make a policeman angry. The scheme was a bold and controversial attempt to improve the quality of leadership in the force. Trenchard was sent to Scotland Yard in 1931 to modernize the force and build up its integrity and morale. In the twenties there had been a series of scandals and it was well known that the standard of most of the senior officers was much lower than it should have been. Trenchard saw no reason why the same ideas which he had employed to successfully in establishing the Royal Air Force should not work just as well in the police. He began by virtually writing off as hopeless the existing superintendents and top commanders. The regulations did not allow him to do what an earlier commissioner, Sir Nevil Macready had done at Scotland Yard when faced with a similar problem, and draft in top commanders from the armed forces. He had to accept that his reforms, drastic as they were, would not begin to have an impact at the top until at least ten years had passed. What concerned him was that the Metropolitan Police should start at once to provide the finest and most modern training for leadership. Hendon opened its doors in the face of fierce criticism from outside. Although Trenchard was strongly supported by the government, his assailants included the Labour Party and practically every serving policeman. What made things worse, from a police viewpoint, was his attempt to introduce, at the same time as Hendon, an ill-fated and badly thought out scheme for short service engagements of constables. Trenchard had incensed police opinion by making slighting references to the senior constables in the force as 'men with nothing to look forward to but their pensions'. He saw the short service scheme as an essential corollary to Hendon. It is only fair to add that Trenchard never sought to make the college exclusive to public schoolboys and graduates and many of the young policemen who were trained there until the outbreak of war were ordinary entrants. But the aura of class prejudice was sufficient to condemn the scheme outright in police eyes, and when Hendon closed for the duration of the war it had few mourners.

When an old and dying Trenchard spoke in the House of Lords in the fifties and advocated that the police should resurrect Hendon, few listened. By this time, the Police College had been established and the service had its own pattern of training for leadership. Trenchard could take some satisfaction in showing that the service which had fought so bitterly against his scheme had been glad enough, after the war, to make so many of his old boys commanders of provincial forces. There was even a feeling of pride in the appointment of Sir Joseph Simpson as the 'first commissioner of the Metropolitan Police to have risen from the ranks of constables'. It was conveniently overlooked that Simpson, like so many of his chief-officer contemporaries, would never have come near a police station had it not been for Hendon.

Until the number of separate police forces was drastically reduced by amalgamations in the sixties, chief officers were divided into two groups, those who had been to Hendon and those who had not. With few exception, there was little fraternizing between the groups. Men like Eric St Johnstone, chief constable of Oxford at the tender age of twenty-nine and afterwards in charge of Durham and Lancashire, Edward Dodd, chief constable of Birmingham, and Simpson had little in common with the rough-hewn professional policeman who had climbed to the top laboriously in their own forces. As a rule, the county chiefs were the Hendon men and well attuned to the hunting, shooting, fishing set. The city and borough chiefs, apart from Dodd, were the ones who had truly risen from the ranks. An interesting exception is Sir Arthur Young, for twenty years until 1971 the commissioner of the City of London force, a unit which would seem to be tailor-made for a Hendon graduate. Young started off as an office boy in Portsmouth police headquarters, made a reputation as a detective and became chief constable of the tiny Leamington Spa force. In common with many younger chief constables of the war period, he became a colonel with the Control Commission in Germany and was three times released by the City of London to perform important police functions outside Britain, in Malaya, in Kenya (where he resigned rather than yield to political pressure on the local police) and as chief of the Royal Ulster Constabulary during the crisis of 1969-70. One of his major concerns during his career has been the building up of the prestige and quality of the Police College, particularly the Special Course.

Young's long police career is all the more remarkable because he has achieved so much success in the face of the powerful challenge from contemporaries who had all the advantages of Hendon. Yet he is in every sense of the word exceptional, and his temperament and approach to police problems is much closer to the Hendon group than to the views of the self-made commanders.

All the Hendon-trained chief officers are now approaching the end of their police careers. Already observers close to the police scene wonder where their successors are to be found. In ten years there should be no problem in finding commanders who have been trained by the Police College, but there is bound to be an interim period when ready-made chief officers will be thin on the ground. Already, there have been some indications of a problem in the offing. A man who was recently appointed to command one of the largest police forces in the country failed, only a few years before, to be selected for a fairly modest post at the Police College, when the interviewing board decided that none of the applicants was of the calibre required and re-advertised the post. Now he commands this very large force which, in addition to being somewhat old-fashioned and in need of firm and inspired leadership, is an uneasy amalgamation of a large county and small boroughs. He is a good policeman with a distinguished record as a practical man, but he would be the first to admit that his command experience was strictly limited before he found himself elevated to his high position. And yet he could also be held up as a shining example of how it is possible for a comparatively young man to reach the top of the promotion ladder in today's police service. He has done it without patronage and without even the modest push provided by accelerated promotion through the college. The question which can only be answered by his performance in the next few years is: 'having got to the top, what does he do there?'

One can hardly overstate the importance of a chief constable in a police force's organization and quality. It so happens that the half-dozen or so chief constables who have, over the past twenty years, been involved in scandals, have all been the self-made men who came up from the bottom. None of the Hendon group has suffered a similar misfortune. It was the coincidence of three such scandals in rapid succession which first raised doubts about the quality of top police leadership in the 1950s. The chief constable of Worcester was gaoled for embezzlement; the chief constable of Brighton was acquitted at the famous conspiracy trial but the judge criticized the leadership he had exercised, and the chief constable of Cardigan was censured following an inquiry into his relations with members of the Police Authority. The Royal Commission on the Police, a few years later, noted that many of the chief constables of the time had never served in another police force and it is now a formal requirement that a chief constable must have had experience outside his own force. This has led to bitter arguments between local Police Authorities and the Home Office when a favoured local man has been rejected. There was some surprise a few years ago when the Police Authority of a large county force, after being told that they could not promote the deputy chief constable, chose as chief constable a man who had commanded a tiny borough force rather than one of the highly fancied names on the short list. The common opinion in the service was that the choice had been dictated more by a determination to spite the Home Office than by the expectional qualities of the successful applicant.

Students of the constitutional position of the police have commented upon the wide discretion that chief constables can exercise in deciding their policies towards certain offences. Traffic is an obvious example. The chief constable of Northampton and County Police happens to be a well-known rally driver. He also disagrees with the 70 mph speed limit. A former chief constable of Buckinghamshire believed, on the contrary, that speeding was a serious offence. Both forces have responsibility for stretches of the M1 motorway and there was an obvious discrepancy between speeding prosecutions in their areas. There was something of an outcry from local shopping interests when a former chief constable of Southend, William Maconnach, announced that henceforth he was not prepared to prosecute shoplifters on behalf of supermarkets whose sales methods were an open invitation to dishonesty. An ex-chief constable of Oxford achieved notoriety in liberal circles for what amounted to a blitz on homosexuals, when most other forces were ignoring all but the most blatant cases of importuning.

Chief constables are not officials of local authorities in the same way as the town clerks and chief medical officers. A Police Authority cannot issue orders to a chief constable on the conduct of particular cases, or on his prosecution policy. Thus the Nottingham Watch Committee was rebuked by the Home Office when it demanded a report from the chief constable on police inquiries which involved local councillors, and the chief constable of Leeds informed his Police Authority that they had no right to propose 'no action' when he informed them that he was prosecuting a local communist for defying a ban on an open-air meeting.

It is their very independence of intrusive local political control which sometimes causes friction between Police Authorities and chief constables. The Metropolitan Commissioner has no such worries. His police authority is the Home Secretary and he has no obligations to a body of councillors. Indeed, ratepayers in London have no representatives to challenge the annual rate precept. The police simply inform the local authorities of how much they will have to pay, although there is token and fairly meaningless consultation with municipal treasurers. Financial control is the one main power of provincial Police Authorities. The forces are funded by equal contributions from the central government and the local authorities. Most of the arguments that arise between chief constables and Police Authorities are related to expenditure. Undoubtedly, some councillors take a perverse delight in trimming the police estimates as their one opportunity to show a chief constable who the bosses are.

'One of the first qualities I would look for in a chief constable,' said a retired one, 'is an ability to stand up to a Town Clerk and a chairman of the Watch Committee. I was always threatening to catch the next train to the Home Office if they were standing in the way of what I needed. It was a way of hinting that the Home Office grant could be stopped.'

'A chief has got to be a strong man,' said a Yorkshire superintendent. 'He's got to be able to get what he wants from his Police Authority, and he's got to be able to keep his senior officers in line. Too many chiefs hand down policy from the top, but they never put themselves out to see if it filters down. If the chief constable never gets out of his office, the commanders below him run the force their way. Give me a chief who says, "This is what I want. Go and do it." Even if he's wrong, the rest of the force knows that it comes from the chief. If the men think that the real power in the force is someone else's, like the deputy chief's, then they lose all respect for the chief constable.'

In 1963, when the Sheffield 'rhino-whip' scandal report was published, the chief constable was criticized for living in an ivory tower and promptly resigned. In that case, his fault was said to have been that he believed implicitly that the false version of events which senior officers had given to him was true, if only because he could not bring himself to believe that men in his force would assault prisoners. The case pinpointed the lonely position of a chief constable. He must at once retain the confidence and support of his men, yet be prepared to probe for signs of malpractice or take the consequences when things go wrong.

In these days of larger forces, few chief constables are able to remain operational policemen, even if they want to be. Their function is increasingly an administrative one, but they must always be aware of what is happening at every level beneath them. This is far from easy, for they command disciplined forces where avenues of approach to senior officers are jealously guarded. In such circumstances, it is perhaps inevitable that a few more chief constables will be discovered in ivory towers. More and more they are having to delegate their leadership functions to the senior officers below them, and the quality of this lower layer of top management in the service takes on an added significance as a result. The force soon learns to identify the name with the real power. 'When you talk about leadership in the police force,' said a Lancashire inspector, 'you're not talking about a man on a horse waving a sword and shouting, "Follow me." You mean a sergeant giving good advice to a probationer, or an inspector sorting out the details of a tricky case to find what offence has been committed, or a superintendent keeping a division together and being sensible in what he expects his men to do. If a man can't take a decision in this job he's not fit for his rank. The trouble is, we've got too many like that.' One of the best known service jokes tells of a superintendent who spent a holiday on a farm. One day he asked the farmer if he could help with the work, and was soon happily engaged in 'muck spreading'. The next day, the farmer took him to the barn and asked him to sort out a pile of apples, putting the large ones in one basket and the small ones in another. That evening the farmer found him sitting disconsolately beside the still empty baskets, with an apple in each hand, moaning, 'Decisions, decisions. . . '

The pace of change in the police service has overtaken some older senior officers. At a time when they could have expected to spend the last few years of their careers comfortably anticipating retirement, they have found themselves involved in a bewildering succession of changes, including new working methods and amalgamations, and the need to adopt a modern management approach. 'The higher-ups made more difficulties about amalgamations than the men on the beat,' said a Yorkshire constable. 'They were too busy feathering their own nests and hanging on to their little empires to give a damn about anyone else. All they were interested in was who was going to be in charge and whether they would have to move into another job.'

'You sometimes look at the top brass in this force and ask yourself how the hell they got there,' said a Midlands constable. 'Half of them wouldn't last five minutes in industry because they've got no initiative of their own and no imagination. They go by the book and instructions from headquarters. The few that aren't like that are bloody good coppers, but the rest . . .'

Just how a senior officer 'got there' is bound up in the promotion system, in itself the source of much discontent in most forces. Although seven out of every ten policemen are constables, the service offers a reasonable prospect of promotion up to the rank of inspector to any officer with the intelligence needed to pass the examinations. As already stated, the Metropolitan Police promotes almost entirely by examination up to the rank of station sergeant.

The rank structure introduced by the first commissioners of the Metropolitan Police in 1829 and adopted by the army officers who commanded the provincial forces in Victorian times, has survived with only a few changes to this day. Originally, each rank corresponded roughly with an army rank, although civilian nomenclatures were used deliberately to avoid any suspicion of militarism in the new police. Oddly enough, the army title of sergeant was left unaltered and has survived several attempts at change. Police sergeants strongly object to being equated by the public with army sergeants, holding that they have far more responsible jobs.

One essential difference between the rank structure and promotion in the police and job advancement in other civilian occupations is the primary function of discipline, or supervision, which is implicit in each rank in the force. In industry and commerce, for example, a man is more likely to be promoted for his professional competence than his potential as a leader of men. The police service is looking for a commander when a man is promoted. Mr John Hill, the assistant commissioner of the Metropolitan Police with responsibility for training and promotion, put this point quite bluntly in an interview with the force's newspaper *The Job* (26 February 1971): 'promotion is not given as a reward for past services, however good. It is given to individuals who appear to have a capacity for growth and greater responsibilities.'

At every level of the police service, it is possible to find men who are disappointed and embittered by their failure to reach a higher rank. I have known officers in the rank of superintendent and above who have regarded the promotion of a colleague as a personal disaster to themselves. This is illustrated by an incident which happened in one of the largest provincial forces a few years ago. The chief constable was expected to retire shortly, and speculation about his successor was rife. The service was surprised when one of the obvious contenders, the youngest of the assistant chief constables in the force, suddenly retired. He was a man of unquestioned ability as a practical policeman and apparently unlimited ambition (which did not exactly endear him to his fellow chief officers). Uncertainty over the future had strained relationships amongst the top brass at headquarters and the chief constable was keeping a tight-lipped silence about the succession. To make matters worse, the chairman and vice chairman of the police authority were at each other's throats and it was common knowledge that any nominee of the one would automatically be opposed by the other. Finally, in an effort to extract at least a hint from the chief constable, this assistant had approached him with an unusual request. He pointed out that he had completed thirty years' service and asked the chief if the police authority would raise any objections to his retiring on pension shortly, rather than when he was sixty in ten years time? Normally, no Police Authority would allow this, but the former assistant told me, 'He just looked up at me and said, "I quite agree with you, — . When you've got as far as you're going to, you might as well get out". I was struck by the fact that this man, who had enjoyed quite spectacular success in his police career, could look back only on this one moment of bitterness when thinking of his hears in the force. For the most part, however, dissatisfaction with promotion is one of the root causes of discontent in the service, which is one of the reasons why the authorities have been paying considerable attention to the whole question of promotion in recent years. In the thirties, a former policeman wrote a book about his experiences as a constable in a very small borough force in the West Riding. One of his characters observed, 'The police force is like a cesspool. The scum rises to the top.' That one phrase made the author famous in police circles. Promotion in those days was riddled with abuses, blatant favouritism and religious prejudice. This was at its worst in the small forces, where one mistake could destroy a man's career.

'I made my mistake during the war,' said a sergeant in a Lancashire force who was on the point of retiring. 'If I thought about it for a bit I could give you the exact date. It was when petrol was rationed of course and during the blackout I followed a car and stopped it. It turned out to be the chief inspector who'd been to see his fancy woman. That was an unauthorized journey and I said I'd report him. I should have known that he'd be able to say that he was on official business. He was a Mason, you see. Well, I wasn't promoted until that man had retired.'

Until the Police Act of 1964, the Watch Committees of city and borough councils had the power to promote policemen. In county forces, this has always been the prerogative of the chief constables. Before 1964 it was not at all uncommon for Watch Committees to overrule recommendations from chief constables in order to promote men who were particular friends of some local councillors. About ten years ago there was a fairly notorious case at Bootle where the chief constable recommended the promotion of an inspector to superintendent. The chief's nominee was a Protestant, but the Labour and mainly Catholic majority on the Watch Committee decided instead to promote a Catholic inspector.

'When I joined the borough force,' said an inspector who is now serving in a large amalgamated force, 'you had to be a Mason to get on. It was as simple as that. I've seen men who could hardly make ends meet at home scrimping and saving to raise the money to get into the Lodge. Believe me, they thought it was worth it, because that's where all the promotions were made.' Whatever else has been achieved by the 1964 Act and the wholesale police amalgamations which followed it a couple of years later, the elimination of patronage and favouritism from police promotion in provincial forces is a real achievement.

During the 1960s there was a series of changes in the promotion regulations designed to encourage the able young careerists in the force. The old regulation prevented a constable from even sitting the promotion examination until he had completed four years service. Now he can take it after two and be eligible for his first promotion (to sergeant) after three. It is just possible for a man to become an inspector with four years' service, but so far only a handful of Bramshill-trained men have done this. Policemen complain, with some justification, that Home Office recruiting publicity which stresses that a man could be an inspector by the time he is twenty-four and a superintendent at thirty is grossly misleading. In 1971 there were just three men who were inspectors at twenty-four and four who were a year older. Only ten officers in the superintendent grades were below thrity-five. It is safe to assume that all were 'high flyers' from Bramshill.

Nevertheless, there is no doubt that police promotion, compared with the snail-like progress made in earlier years, is now meteoric. The large and rapid rise in the numbers of policemen has increased the opportunities. Chief officers have followed a general policy of filling each vacancy in the ranks above constable, even though there may be a huge shortage of men. This has meant, of course, that the number of promotions has been disproportionate, because the number of each rank in a force should be related to the establishment. One result has been that in some forces there is a danger of the promotion channel becoming blocked with younger officers waiting impatiently for the superiors to move over. To quote the Metropolitan's Mr Hill again: 'For several years conditions have been too favourable and promotion, in some instances, has come too easily. . In this force a year or two ago an inspector felt he was missing the boat if he had not been promoted by the time he had four years in the rank. Now he is lucky even to be considered before he has this much service.' The Metropolitan is one of those which has had to slow down its promotion rate, mainly because so many younger officers have been promoted and bottlenecks at each level on the rank structure have built up; this is in spite of the fact that the Metropolitan has lower ages of compulsory retirement for senior officers than the provinces, and sticks to the rules (in spite of the protests of the Superintendent's Association) in order to keep the promotion flow moving. An added problem facing all forces in the early 1970s is the fact that, because there was no recruitment during the war years, fewer officers are now eligible to retire.

Problems of this kind, however, affect only a small part of the force. They frustrate the ultra-ambitious and thwart the plans of chief officers to bring forward young top-rankers. But the emphasis on youth for its own sake which has been so evident in the plans for higher training and accelerated promotion has had a much greater effect on the rest of the service, where resentment against high flyers has been building up ever since the Special Course began. 'This automatic promotion to inspector when they've only been back from the college a year is all wrong,' said a Devon sergeant. 'I can tell you that we have one on our section and I'm having to carry him. He's a nice enough lad but he's never been a policeman and he never will be one. He might know a lot about law, but he can't tell men what to do because he can't do it himself.' This sergeant may have been expressing a personally jaundiced viewpoint, but I have heard similar remarks up and down the country about the lack of practical ability of Bramshill-trained inspectors. It may be nothing more than understandable jealousy of the privileged position of younger men who appear set for rapid promotion, but the police service has always placed a unique value on practical experience.

'They tell us that there's plenty of room for the Bramshill types,' said a chief inspector in the Midlands. 'I know that about forty a year don't make all that much difference to promotions to inspector. But you've got to look ahead. There aren't many senior ranks as it is, and if these men are going to be pushed to the top, simply because they've got the backing of the Home Office, it's a bloody poor look-out for the rest of us.'

'I went for extended interviews at Eastbourne for the Special Course,' a Lancashire sergeant told me. 'I wasn't selected, and as I was nearly thirty at the time I knew they thought I was a bit old. But it was getting so near, and then being turned down. It's not really the course you're being selected for, it's your whole future. In a few years time, there won't be many men getting to the top if they haven't been on the course.'

A chief constable, on the other hand, thought that there was a real danger of the Bramshill scheme's importance in the promotion system becoming grossly exaggerated. 'You must realize that all that Bramshill can do for a man is give him his automatic promotion to inspector after he's been back in his force for a year. After that, he's just another inspector. He went to the college because, at the time he was interviewed, it was thought that he had the potential to rise to senior rank relatively quickly. Let's assume that this was correct. He still has to demonstrate, by his work as an inspector, that he is entitled to be made a chief inspector or a superintendent. I certainly would not promote him just because he's been on the Special Course.'

The Special Course, it is true, is but one small part of the overall promotion system. As already mentioned, the system has been the subject of intensive internal study in recent years. The Royal Commission on the Police refrained in its report from lengthy comments, mainly because the Committee on Higher Police Training, set up in 1959, was at work. In 1965, however, the Police Federation produced a document, called 'The Problem', which was extremely critical of the promotion system and, in particular, what it regarded as attempts to 'glorify rank' at the expense of the constable's status. This, in turn, led to a report on management by the Police Advisory Board which said: 'It is probable that failure to appraise men properly for promotion by putting too much weight on their qualities as policemen and too little on their potential as leaders, has in the past had adverse effects on the service. Aptitude for leadership should be regarded as one of the major considerations in deciding whether a police officer should be promoted.' The Board made these remarks in the context of undeniable evidence that there was a great deal of bad management of men in the police. This is a disciplined service, where obedience to orders is the first obligation of a subordinate. When a policeman is promoted he assumes a disciplinary responsibility over those below him, and if he is autocratic or lacks human understanding he can make life miserable for them. In the years when the service offered a man security against widespread unemployment outside, petty tyranny just had to be tolerated. What the Police Advisory Board was faced with was clear evidence that men had left the police in recent years because they were not prepared to be treated in this fashion. All the same, the suggestion that it was possible to put 'too much weight on qualities as policemen' raised quite a few eyebrows in the force. Take a typical case. J joined the force nearly twenty years ago, straight from national service in the army. He passed all the examinations at the first attempt and is now qualified, on paper, for promotion to inspector. He is still a constable and has realized for some years now that he will probably retire as one. J has just one hope left, that he might be one of the few long-service constables who are made sergeants each year, as part of the force policy of giving a little encouragement to men like J and, at the same time, making sure that the promotion channel is not blocked by promoting too many young men. J is regarded by his colleagues as a good policeman. In his time he has caught many thieves and has been commended for outstanding police work on three occasions, once by a High Court judge. Early in his service, he was selected for the CID and did quite well. He asked to revert to the uniformed branch, however, at a time when his wife was ill and he needed to spend more time at home than a conscientious detective could expect to devote to his domestic affairs. Perhaps it was this decision to put his family before his job that has weighed against him ever since. J does not know, because he has never been given a reason. Twice he has been told, unofficially, that the promotion board has recommended him and three times he had had a long and friendly interview with the chief constable on the subject. On these occasions, he has waited eagerly for good news which has never arrived.

Of half a dozen men who joined the force at the same time as he did, J has seen two rise to superintendent and two to inspector. As constables, they were all close friends. (He was best man at two of their weddings and one of the superintendents was godfather to his son.) His wife was friendly with the other wives, the families visited each other frequently and sometimes shared holidays. As his colleagues have moved up the ladder, however, the friendships have died away. There are no visits any more, just the occasional 'Hows's the family?' enquiry from a superior officer to a subordinate. J insists that he is not jealous of other people's success, just bitter about what has happened to him. What he resents more than anything is that men who joined the force years after he did, men who used to come for advice to him, are now his superiors.

If his wife had her way, J would not now be a policeman. For some years she has asked him on many occasions to look for another job. With his fortieth birthday behind him, she realizes that he might as well wait until he has completed the twenty-five years' service that will give him a half-pay pension. J will admit that he has often thought about leaving the police. With no special skills and no real knowledge of any other kind of job, however, he has settled for security, and the certainty of his pension. Many men in his position have virtually lost interest in their job, but not J. He remains a dedicated policeman, respected by his colleagues and popular with the local community.

If his chief constable was to be asked to explain why J has not been promoted, no doubt his reasons would be sound. The chief might, for instance, believe that he is a first class constable who would not be able to carry the extra responsibility of rank. Or it might be that the chief has never been able to see in him the potential to rise to higher rank, and the policy in promoting a man is to open the way for him to move further. J might remain a sergeant and block a promotion channel. The chief is a great believer in young men being given their heads.

This question of age takes on a new significance in the modern police service. Little more than ten years ago, promotion in the police depended upon experience and seniority more than ability and obvious potential. A man was considered to be doing well if he was promoted to sergeant with less than ten years' service, and he was expected to gain a lot of experience in that rank before moving up. It was very much a case of waiting, if not for dead men's shoes, then for time-expired senior officers to retire. Now the emphasis has changed completely. The rapid increase in the size of the service has meant, naturally, that there are many more posts to fill. The most important factor has been the radical change in promotion policy, made necessary by the development of higher training. This is based on the theory that, if the service is to continue to provide its future leaders from within its own ranks, it has got to catch them young.

J and his generation of policemen have been overtaken by the change, and many of them resent what has happened. Whatever the faults of a promotion system which seemed to be based on experience and seniority, it appeared to them to be much fairer than one which allows the youngsters in the service to leapfrog over them. They joined a police service in which accelerated promotion and superintendents of thirty were unheard of, now they know that some men are too old for the Police College if they have more than ten years' service. Whatever the benefits modern thinking on promotion may bring to the younger policeman, those who joined the service too soon will never become reconciled to it. To J, Mr John Hill's statement that promotion is not 'a reward for past services, however good' but given to those who 'appear to have a capacity for growth and greater responsibilities' offers no encouragement.

'There are, generally speaking, such things as promotion fields in the police force for each rank,' said the former chief constable. 'You can say that if a man is to go high in the service his first promotion to sergeant must come quickly, and he mustn't spend too much time there before he becomes an inspector. After that, he moves into another field for chief inspector and then superintendent. According to his age and length of service he either has a great future in front of him or he has, frankly, missed the boat.'

At one time transfer on promotion to another force was very exceptional. The Royal Commission on the Police recommended that one chief inspector's vacancy in every three should be advertised. Some chief constables went much further than this and advertised for sergeants, much to the resentment of their own men who were qualified for promotion. Since the amalgamations have provided chief constables with a much wider choice, the number of advertised vacancies has dropped considerably.

The fact that the existing system of promotion had many defects was summed up in the comment of the Police Advisory Board's working party on Operational Efficiency and Management;* 'failure to appraise men properly for promotion . . . has in the past had adverse effects on the service . . . ' An interesting attempt to remedy this situation was the Report, published in 1971, of the Advisory Board's working party on Staff Appraisal in the police.

*Police Manpower, Equipment and Efficiency, London, 1967.

The Report gave five main objectives of staff appraisal: to assess the manner in which an officer is carrying out his duties; to discover his capabilities; to see whether he is being employed on the kind of work most suited to him; to identify officers suitable for promotion 'including young officers worthy of advancement', and to identify an officer's training needs. Of these objectives, promotion is the most important as far as the police themselves are concerned.

The working party recommended a system of annual reports on every officer in the lower ranks. Staff appraisal could have a strong influence on future promotions in forces where chief officers have adopted the system. The annual report is intended to give a full picture of an officer, pointing out his strengths and weaknesses. Unusually, in a service where reports on individual officers have always been wrapped in secrecy, the scheme insists that a report, which must be prepared frankly, must be shown to the officer or else he must be informed of its contents, and that he must be given the chance to discuss any criticisms, at an interview with his divisional commander. The Report accepts that few police officers will have any real understanding of the techniques of staff appraisal and proposes initial training for this purpose.

The appraisal report is usually in three parts. The first takes the form of a grid and assesses how the man copes with his duty; the second part compares his performance with those of his colleagues; the third is a description of the officer as an individual. The Advisory Board report concludes with this warning:

Staff appraisal is not without its dangers. Experience in America has shown that antagonism to those who report, by those reported upon, can have a serious effect on the efficiency of an organization. This can only be overcome by the acceptance of the scheme by all involved and the careful training of those who are to operate the scheme. Staff appraisal in the police service should be designed to ensure job satisfaction and full use of the talents of the individual.

Perhaps it will, but soon after the report was published it was clear that resistance to staff appraisal was perhaps stronger than the authors of the report had anticipated. In the lower ranks there was suspicion about a system which envisaged regular checks on the work performance of the police. One chief officer in a very large force reassured doubters in his command by dismissing the report as 'a load of bloody nonsense'. He was quite satisfied with his existing system of promotion and reports on officers.

No one could seriously maintain that even the most efficient system of staff appraisal would banish all the grumbles about promotion in the police. But at least it would give to officers like J, at present unable to find any clue to the reason for years of disappointment and rejection, some indication of why he has never made it.

And, as the Lancashire constable put it to me, 'The worst thing is not knowing why . . . '

7 Discipline, complaints, public relations

In 1969, a total of 10,647 complaints were made against the police in England and Wales. After investigation, it was decided by the police that in the overwhelming majority of cases there was either no justification for the complaint or the facts did not disclose a breach of duty by the policeman concerned. The Chief Inspector of Constabulary said in his annual report for 1969 that, out of 7,351 complaints made against provincial police officers, only 988 were substantiated, and disciplinary proceedings were instituted in only 153 cases. The Metropolitan commissioner recorded a grand total of 3,296 complaints but omitted to say how many were held to be groundless. However, disciplinary proceedings were instituted in fifty-five cases.

The bald figures are interesting. They represent a ratio of one complaint to every nine policemen in England and Wales, yet only 158 officers, or less than two in every thousand, faced a police disciplinary charge arising out of a complaint. This is either a tribute to the generally immaculate behaviour of the police or clear evidence that there will never be a guarantee of satisfaction for complainants until the police cease to have control of the investigation procedure.

The total of complaints has been rising by approximately ten per cent every year since 1965, the first year in which the police were obliged by the Police Act to record and investigate every complaint, no matter how trivial. At first sight the total of over 10,000 complaints in 1969 is disturbing, until it is related to the size of the force and the whole of the year. A policeman is on duty for about 230 days a year, making a very round figure of twenty-one million working days for the force as a whole, during which there were only these ten thousand or so incidents which resulted in a formal complaint. A startling incidental statistic is the Metopolitan commissioner's information that chief inspectors in London spent over 10,000 man-hours in 1969 investigating complaints.

How good or bad are present relations between the police and the public?

C. H. Rolph, besides being a well-known. writer and criminologist, is a retired policeman and, as such, is uniquely qualified to comment on the role of the police in society. In 1962, when the Royal Commission on the Police was investigating all aspects of police and public relationships he wrote:

It is difficult, in assessing police and public relationships, not to be swayed by the last few opinions one has heard or read. When 'police violence' for example, is under discussion there is noticeable a clear-cut class attitude. The Top People tend to the view that if a man cuts up rough with the police and gets hurt, he has asked for and deserved what he got. (I find this view particularly prevalent among leading lawyers.) The middle-class citizen tends to disbelieve all such stories, and is thus able fairly comfortably to dismiss them but is deeply shocked when one of them is proved true. The proles accept them as self-evidently true and are genuinely surprised at any expression of doubt. The same is true of corruption, and perjury, and other less clearly occupational lapses like burglary and fraud.*

How true is this analysis of class attitudes to police misconduct? It has always been accepted that the Top People and the middle classes are the natural allies of the policeman. Some might say, with a touch of cynicism, that it is the other way round, that the police have always ingratiated themselves with their betters. After all, the police service grew out of the determination of the wealthy to protect themselves from the worst excesses of the lower orders. The strongest encourage-

* *The Police and the Public* (London 1962).

ment to the formation of a new police force was the prevailing lawlessness of Britain in the aftermath of the Napoleonic wars and the inability of the old watchmen to protect life and property. To this was added the anxiety of the mill and mine owners, the iron-masters and the rest to safeguard their growing industrial affluence both from criminals and the restlessness of working people. The laws passed in those years had the same purpose, to sanctify property and punish those whose activities might challenge the social order. In this policy, the middle classes looked to the police for effective support and got it. Throughout the nineteenth century, the police would always be found in enthusiastic support of the property owners against the demonstrators, strikers, and impoverished tenants. The in-bred hostility of the working classes of those years has to some extent survived in working-class attitudes towards the police today. The Labour Government of 1964-70 evoked little enthusiasm among its supporters for its comprehensive programme of police reform, involving an unprecedented increase in the numbers of police and a trebling of expenditure. The Conservatives, on the other hand, used the 'law and order' issue in the build-up to their successful campaign in 1970, with the implication that Labour did not support the police, in the sure knowledge that they would strike a responsive chord in middle-class breasts.

And yet it might not be wholly accurate to define 'clear-cut' class attitudes towards the police in the way that Rolph described them in 1962. Particularly in relation to police misconduct, it is the articulate middle class which has led the agitation for, for example, a system of independent investigation of complaints against the police. The case for this has been argued not by trade unions angered by strike-breaking but by groups of lawyers, notably 'Justice', the Society of Labour Lawyers, and even the Inns of Court Conservative Association. All these bodies have added their weight to the constant theme of the National Council for Civil Liberties, and the limited successes which have been achieved in this direction have shown that authority is more susceptible to middle-class pressure than all the agitation and complaints which used to be made by working-class politicians and trade unions.

Recent years have seen significant shifts in public opinion of the police, and nowhere is this more marked than among the middle classes. A popular explanation of the fact that many middle-class people now seem to be less favourably inclined towards the police is the impact of the motor car on what was once a comfortable, though (on the police side) forelock-tugging, relationship. The motoring public, or at least a large and vociferous section of it, stubbornly refuses to equate motoring offences with law-breaking and regards police enforcement of traffic law as persecution. Even middle-class standards of sportsmanship come into the argument. When radar speed traps were introduced, the motoring organizations protested that the police were not playing the game. A similar argument was used when some police forces decided to patrol stretches of dangerous roads with unmarked police vehicles. The solid citizen who supports a petition for a 30mph speed limit in his village high street is the same man who will feel outraged if he is caught in a radar trap doing 50mph through someone else's village. He is the man most likely to write to the chief constable and become yet another statistic in the annual total of complaints. Using traffic wardens to supervise street parking has not only relieved the police of one of the jobs they detested, it has created another target for the motorist's wrath. Some advocates of the complete separation of the police from traffic responsibilities argue that, as this is the most thankless task the police perform, it would be better to hand everything over to a traffic corps and leave the police free to concentrate on crime, where they could be sure of the support of the law-abiding public.

It is not only traffic, however, which has made deep inroads upon traditional middle-class support for the police. A superintendent who is deeply involved in public relations in his force told me: 'The police have become a kind of uniformed embodiment of the ordinary man's frustration. He feels that this country is so regulated with laws telling him what he cannot do, that when a policeman comes along to tell him he mustn't do something, he gets angry. But he's not really getting at the policeman, he's shouting at all authority. He's fed up of being pushed around.'

Another senior officer said, 'As an ordinary individual, I'm surprised by the number of officials of this and that who now have a statutory right to come into my house. Apart from the gas board and the electricity people, do you realise that there are all kinds of people in local and central government who can come in? It's not so much that they all do, but the knowledge that Parliament has passed all these laws. Try putting up a garden shed without permission, or altering your house in any way. There's always someone who can come along and tell you that you can't do it. So is it surprising that more people get touchy if they don't like a copper's tone of voice?'

A Midlands senior officer felt that there was a close relationship between publicity and the incidence of complaints. He said: 'After one story about an immigrant being hit by a policeman appeared in the *Birmingham Mail* the rate of complaints in a week shot up. It's always the same, the publicized complaint has a bandwagon effect. People who are anti-police write to the papers, reporters go round the district looking for people with a grievance and drag up incidents that have never even been reported.' The result is that the ratio of complaints goes up, and because the lads are annoyed by the publicity and the cockiness of the West Indians, some are bound to be genuine. It's all a matter of cause and effect. If you keep saying that police-public relationships are rotten, they very soon will be.'

Any survey of the regular bulletins of the National Council for Civil Liberties or the other bodies which assist people with grievances would suggest that there is no room for complacency about the general behaviour of the police in the community. 'Release', a body set up to assist young people involved in drug charges, has been especially vehement in its attacks on police practices, and a similar line is taken by militant bodies representing, or claiming to represent, immigrant interests. With so many pressure-groups at work in the capital, it is not altogether surprising that the Metropolitan policeman has something like a three-to-one better chance of being involved in a complaint than his provincial colleague.

The fact that the police reject such a high proportion of complaints as unfounded (eighty-six per cent of complaints in provincial forces were so rejected in 1969) would seem to lend support for the allegations of police whitewashing which such bodies as the NCCL make so often. The Chief Inspector of Constabulary said in his annual report for 1969 that the opportunity had been taken to seek out information relating to those cases where the complainant had made some formal representation of dissatisfaction with the investigation or its outcome. There were 151 such cases in 1969, or a little over two per cent. The Chief Inspector drew from this the following conclusion: 'These figures speak for themselves and bear testimony to the thorough and fair manner in which all complaints received are dealt with by chief officers of police.' To which opponents of the present system of wholly internal police investigations would retort that the Chief Inspector produced no comparable figures of complainants who expressed satisfaction with the outcome; that in any case complainants are never fully informed of the action taken, even in cases where disciplinary proceedings follow a complaint; and that the majority of complainants never really expected that their complaint would be properly dealt with to their satisfaction. Perhaps more reliable statistics given by the Chief Inspector of Constabulary are those which refer to the 1,325 (or eighteen per cent) of the total of complaints in which the complainant indicated a wish not to proceed with the allegation. It has long been evident to investigating officers that many members of the public are genuinely appalled by the consequences of a complaint, sometimes made in the heat of the moment, particularly when they have to make a statement to a senior police officer, answer questions, and are warned to attend any disciplinary inquiry that may be held.

'We often get the type who comes rushing into the station after he's had a few words with a policeman, perhaps about his car,' said a chief inspector in London. 'We give the leaflet on how to make a complaint. If he's cooled down enough to read it, he often tells us to forget it there and then. But he might make a statement. That's when he tells you that he doesn't want to get the policeman into trouble. What he really wants is someone at the police station to agree with him and tell the constable not to speak to him like that. It's only a few who want their pound of flesh by seeing the constable punished.'

Contrary to opinions expressed in non-police circles, the police do go to great lengths to ensure that a complaint from the public is properly investigated. It may have been true to say, a few years ago, that complainants were chased out of police stations by irate sergeants threatening to put them in the cells if they did not clear off, but the shadow of the Sheffield 'rhino-whip' affair in 1963 still hangs over the whole question of complaints, as a sinister reminder of what can happen to senior officers when allegations are not investigated properly. The Sheffield case was the main reason why the Police Act of 1964 imposed statutory obligations on chief officers to investigate every complaint.

It was a shocking and sordid story, both in its disclosures of police violence and in the frantic attempts made by the police to cover up the facts. The story began with some members of the CID being formed into a special squad to deal with a spate of crime in the city. Although senior officers denied it, it seems clear now that the squad was told to get results and that no one would be too particular as to how they were obtained. One immediate result was the arrest of three men with criminal records. At the police station they were interrogated by two young detectives and it was afterwards alleged that they were beaten up and threatened with the 'rhino-whip'. When they appeared in court the next morning, after being kept in custody overnight, their solicitor immediately complained that they were injured and had been assaulted by the police. An inquiry was ordered. Then began the elaborate 'cover-up' operation. As the official inquiry afterwards reported: 'We are convinced that... apart from the chief constable, no one really wanted to investigate the truth.' The chief superintendent in charge of the CID told the inquiry, 'The allegations were being made by hardened persistent criminals and I believed the leaders of the crime squad long before them.' It was an understandable, if ill-advised, reaction on the part of a senior officer. Nothing is more calculated to undermine morale in the force than a suggestion that policemen cannot rely on the support of their superiors when complained against by criminals.

The men's solicitor took a different view. He believed that there was clear evidence that his clients had been brutally assaulted in police custody and demanded that the force should prosecute those responsible. He was told by the chief constable that he could either bring a prosecution himself, as a private person, or leave the matter in the hands of the police who would hold a disciplinary investigation. By this time, the local newspaper was giving the case publicity and demanding answers to embarrassing questions. Local MPs were showing an interest. As there was still no sign of any police action, the solicitor launched, on behalf of the men, a private prosecution against the two young detectives.

There are many such prosecutions during a year. Usually they take the form of cross-summonses issued by persons charged with assaulting the police. Invariably, they are dismissed by the magistrates who prefer the evidence of the police officers concerned. On this occasion, to the great surprise of everyone in court, the policemen admitted the charges. Through a barrister, they explained in mitigation that they had been provoked by the prisoners, who had fought among themselves and attacked the police. They strongly denied using a 'rhino-whip'. The magistrates, no doubt accepting that this was an unfortunate case in which two young officers had indeed been provoked and had overstepped the bounds, fined them. But, if the story their lawyer advanced was correct, why had they pleaded guilty? If policemen have to use force to restrain violent prisoners, a court will nearly always acquit them of charges brought by private prosecutors. The conclusion is inescapable that the officers took this course on advice from higher up. One of the advantages of pleading guilty is that there can be no rebuttal by the prosecution of anything said in mitigation. The assaulted prisoners were not able to give evidence. In this way, some senior officers in the Sheffield force hoped that the matter would immediately be forgotten.

When a police officer is convicted by a court, the question of his retention in the force arises. The two detectives appeared in front of the chief constable, who had no inkling of the truth, and were dismissed from the force. This decision came as a shock to the men, and probably to their CID superiors who may have expected the chief constable to make allowances for provocation. Now out of a job and with their police careers ruined, the detectives realized that they had been left holding the buck. Their reaction was to protest in public. Now they said that they had acted on orders, and that they had indeed assaulted the prisoners in an effort to get confessions. From being a local matter, the case suddenly assumed the proportions of a major scandal.

When the detectives gave notice of appeal against dismissal from the force, the Home Secretary (Mr Henry Brooke) took the unprecedented step of announcing that the appeal tribunal, under a distinguished lawyer, would sit in public. It was obvious that the inquiry was hardly concerned with the question of whether two detectives who admitted that they had beaten up prisoners should be reinstated in the force. The real issue was the degree of culpability of the rest of the force. In their evidence, the detectives insisted that they were acting on orders and that senior officers were either present or close by when the assaults occurred. The tribunal's report found that all this was substantially true. Some senior officers promptly resigned and shortly afterwards the chief constable left the service. His failure had been to place too implicit a trust in his senior officers. He simply could not believe that they would supply him with a wholly false explanation of what had taken place. It was a failure that cost him his job, but not one that would lose him the respect of his colleagues in the force.

Sheffield, it almost goes without saying, was in every way an exceptional case. It was exceptional because, contrary to some beliefs, beatings are not routine CID procedure. It was exceptional because of the complete failure of the senior officers, from the top downwards, to face their responsibilities of investigation and discipline. And it was exceptional in another sense, for the fact that, in the end, senior and junior officers suffered alike for their misdeeds or sins of omission.

The 'rhino-whip' case did real harm to the police service. There was the predictable middle-class reaction that C.H. Rolph had only just written of: '. . . the middle-class citizen tends to disbelieve all such stories . . . but is deeply shocked when one of them is proved true'. The National Council for Civil Liberties and others had a field-day, arguing that this case was just the tip of the iceberg. The press went into an orgy of self-congratulation, giving all the credit to the local editor and the lawyer for their determination to expose the facts. In reality, there would never have been a public inquiry if the dismissed detectives had been content to take the entire blame. It was because they felt betrayed by their superiors that they changed their stories. It took the Sheffield force years to live down the shame of the affair. Even in 1970, a barrister made an attack on the force at Sheffield Assizes. A client had made allegations against the police, and the barrister urged the jury to remember that such things happened in Sheffield. Afterwards, he felt it right to make an apology in open court for making an unfounded attack. Oddly enough, he was the same barrister who had defended the detectives at the magistrate's court.

The Sheffield case was embarrassing for the police in another way. Less than a year earlier the Royal Commission on the Police had rejected all the proposals for an independent investigation of complaints system, saying that they were confident that internal investigations were both thorough and fair. Here was a classic example of how the police could, if so minded, cover up the truth. Hard on the heels of the Sheffield case came the Challenor scandal, in which this London detective sergeant and three young constables were charged with 'planting' half-bricks on a group of people arrested at a political demonstration, as evidence to support charges of possessing offensive weapons. The significance of the Challenor case will be discussed in a later chapter, but here was yet another instance where it appeared that leaving the investigation of complaints in police hands was far from satisfactory

In the circumstances, it is surprising that the Police Act did not grasp the nettle of the investigation procedure more firmly than merely to insist that all complaints should be recorded and investigated, and that all allegations of a criminal nature should be referred to the Director of Public Prosecutions. The explanation might lie in Henry Brooke's policies at the Home Office. He was not the man to make any gesture which might be regarded as capitulation to the National Council for Civil Liberties. In this he was reinforced by the strong pressure against independent investigations exerted by the Police Federation and, of course, he could quote the views of the Royal Commission on the Police.

The police case against independent investigations is a strong one and it is too often dismissed by those whose obsession with the principle that justice must be seen to be done leads them into too slight a regard for doing justice to the police. For a start, it is important to remember that Sheffield and Challenor cases occur very infrequently. Only someone who refuses to believe anything good of the police would argue that malpractices of this kind are the rule, not the exception. This said, it must be realized that the citizen with a genuine grievance against the police can seek a remedy, including compensation, in the civil courts. As this applies to all the cases where assault is alleged, it cannot be said that access to an independent inquiry is denied to any victim of alleged police brutality. If the complaint alleges that a policeman has broken the law, such as in a case of theft, assault, or perjury, then the question of prosecution is decided not by the police, but by the independent Director of Public Prosecutions. While he must rely on a police investigation, he can and does examine every such report thoroughly, and is able to require further inquiries to be made. The regulations also permit chief officers to request that a complaint from a member of the public be investigated by a senior officer from another force and, to ensure a measure of independence in all investigations, no complaint can be investigated by an officer who is serving in the same department or division of the force as the officer involved in the case.

All these procedures were introduced in the Police Act in an effort to ensure, if not that there were to be no more Sheffields or Challenors, then at least that there would be strong safeguards. The civil libertarians, lawyers and journalists who have raised the issue of independent surveillance of complaints on so many occasions have not been satisfied by the changes, but they do appear to have shifted their ground recently. From arguing that police inquiries led to cover-up operations, they now say that as long as investigations remain entirely in police hands, no matter how honest and impartial they may be, the public will never be convinced that justice is being done.

If chief constables are to be criticized for being too ready to dismiss complaints as unsubstantiated, it is interesting to note that the Director of Public Prosecutions appears to take a similar attitude to allegations of criminal behaviour by policemen. In 1969 he examined 1,255 reports about police officers and criminal proceedings were taken in only 162, of which all but thirteen were road traffic cases.

The police say that independent investigations are impracticable and undesirable. They claim that only trained and experienced policemen can investigate complaints against the police, because only they know what constitutes correct police action and understand proper procedure. A guilty policeman, the argument goes, would find it much easier to hoodwink an independent investigator than a senior policeman. Independent inquiries are undesirable, in police eyes, because they suggest a lack of trust in the ability and willingness of the police to deal with their defaulters. What is more, they regard it as essential that a policeman should know that his conduct is being judged on professional standards by policemen; men who understand the pressures and provocation to which a policeman can be subjected in his daily work.

The argument has gone on, more or less continually, for the last ten years. In 1962 the Royal Commission recommended little change in the *status quo*, although three of their number wanted the appointment of a Commissioner of Rights to look into complaints. In 1968, the then Home Secretary asked his Police Advisory Board to look into the problem, in response to the promptings of backbenchers and others. The Advisory Board represents the Home Office, the Police Authorities and the service organizations, including the Police Federation, so that this was virtually an internal examination of the question. They recommended that either the complainant, the chief officer or the officer concerned should be able to opt for the report of an investigation to be sent to an independent solictor who would decide whether to advise that disciplinary proceedings be taken.

As this relatively minor change would have excluded any outside agency from taking part in investigations or inquiries, it was unlikely to satisfy the critics of the system.* Be that as it may, popular opinion in the police-service is that nowadays

---

*The Home Secretary (Mr R. Maudling) told Parliament in December 1971 that this recommendation was unworkable.

far too much attention is paid to trivial complaints. 'I've had to answer three or four complaints,' said a Lancashire constable. 'Each time I've had the feeling that the force was looking for a way to get me into trouble. They don't ever let you see the actual letter of complaint. All you get is a form which tells you that you might have done something wrong and might be put on a charge. Then they tell you to put your version in writing. Each time it's been something or nothing, really, like swearing at a motorist or threatening to punch someone. I've given them my side of it, and later on you're told that no further action is taken. But I haven't seen what they've said to the bloke that complained. For all I know, they've agreed with him, and it's on my personal file. It gets you down at the time, you worry about what's going to happen.'

Policemen complain that the force now goes to ridiculous lengths to observe the procedures laid down in the Act. The requirement is that every complaint, no matter how trivial, shall be investigated. Some classic examples have emerged. An off-duty policeman threw a lump of earth at a marauding cat in his garden. The next-door neighbour wrote to the chief constable to complain. The policeman was served with a notice suggesting that he might have committed an act likely to discredit the force. A policewoman popped a toffee in her mouth and dropped the wrapper in the gutter. She was reported for a suspected breach of the Litter Act. Perhaps the crowning lunacy was a case in Sussex (under a previous chief constable) where a row over a children's squabble led a policeman to order out of his house the mother-in-law of the policeman who lived next door. He was disciplined for 'being uncivil to a member of the public' and required to resign as an alternative to dismissal. The man appealed to the Home Office, who showed what they thought of the matter by ordering his immediate reinstatement.

'I know that carrying out the law to the letter might look a little ridiculous,' said a chief constable, 'but what else can a chief officer do? He can't write to a complainant to tell him that his complaint is a load of rubbish and not worth looking into.'

The procedure for dealing with officers who are placed on discipline charges as a result of a complaint from the member of the public is the same as that laid down for dealing with all offences against the Police Discipline Regulations. The complainant has a right to be present at the inquiry to give evidence, and may put questions to the accused officer through the chief constable. He cannot be legally represented (neither can the officer) but in some cases may be assisted by a non-legal 'friend'. He has to be informed in general terms of the result, that is whether or not his allegation has been upheld.

A police disciplinary inquiry closely resembles a court of law. The chief constable presides to hear the evidence, reach a verdict, and announce the punishment. The case is presented by a senior police officer who, strictly speaking, is not a prosecutor (he is termed the 'presenting' officer) but whose duty is to put all the known facts before the inquiry. The accused officer can either conduct his own defence or be assisted by a 'friend', invariably a member of the Police Federation with experience in such matters. Witnesses are not sworn, but the rules of evidence are followed as closely as possible.

The inquiry is the ultimate stage in the police discipline procedure before the appeal machinery is brought into use. In 1969 approximately eight hundred policemen appeared before disciplinary inquiries, and something like three quarters of these cases were strictly internal matters. The Home Office circular which explains the Discipline Regulations and procedure stresses that: 'Nothing in the regulations disturbs the established practice of disposing of small matters without recourse to a disciplinary hearing, i.e., by word of caution or admonition from a senior officer.' In fact the number of actual disciplinary charges each year appears to be declining, in spite of the big increase in the number of policemen. All the same, when it is remembered that every complaint originates as a possible breach of discipline and involves the serving of the preliminary warning notice on the officer concerned, it will be appreciated that disciplinary procedures play a considerable part in police administration.

If there is one thing that sets a policeman apart from any other walk of civilian life, it is the Police Discipline Code which, in its sixteen clauses, broken down into twenty-five sub-sections, covers every conceivable sin of omission or commission that it is possible for an officer to be guilty of. The closest analogy to the Discipline Code is to be found in the regulations governing discipline in the armed forces. The code deals with such offences as disobedience to orders, including failure or neglect to carry out any lawful order, and omitting to notify a chief officer of a business interest. This clause also covers any breach of the restrictions placed on the private lives of police officers. Another clause deals with oppressive or abusive conduct by one policeman towards another, or an assault on a colleague. In practice, it is rarely invoked. Neglect of duty is split into several categories: failing to attend to matters within a policeman's responsibilities; not working his beat in accordance with orders; being absent from or late for duty. Falsehood or prevarication is a specific offence, which includes the making of a false report, altering official documents, or making a false statement to secure appointment to the force. It is an offence against discipline to make an improper disclosure of information which a policeman has in his possession as a member of the force; to write an anonymous letter to a Police Authority or a member of the force; or to approach any member of a police authority on a police matter. In this connection, the chief constable of the West Yorkshire force warned the local branch of the Police Federation about approaching councillors in support of the national pay claim in 1970.

Corruption is dealt with in the code in various ways. A policeman must account promptly and properly for any money or property received by him in the course of his duty; he must not solicit or accept any gratuity, present, subscription or testimonial (this has been used on many occasions to ban retirement collections for village policemen); he must not be under a pecuniary obligation to any person in such a manner as might affect his duties; he must not use his position as a policeman to his private advantage; he must not give any other person a reference or character-recommendation without his chief constable's consent. He must not abuse his authority by making an unlawful arrest, using violence to a prisoner or a member of the public, or being uncivil. He must not neglect his health, defined in this clause as not carrying out a doctor's advice or acting, when off duty through sickness, in a manner calculated to impair his recovery and retard his return to duty. He must not be improperly dressed or untidy while in uniform. He must not damage police property either wilfully or through neglect. He must not be unfit for duty through drink (whether on or off duty at the time), nor must he drink on duty without permission and he must never ask anyone to buy him a drink. He must not enter a public house in uniform, even if he is off duty, without 'good and sufficient cause', for which an unquenchable thirst would not qualify. It is an offence against discipline to have been convicted by a court of a criminal offence, which includes a traffic violation.

Just in case an officer is so original as to commit an offence not specifically covered by the Discipline Code, there is always the all-embracing clause of discreditable conduct, which offence is committed where a member of a police force acts in a disorderly manner or any manner prejudicial to discipline, or reasonably likely to bring discredit on the reputation of the force or the police service. This clause is capable of such a wide interpretation that one wonders why the others are included in the code. Many of the offences listed in the code have their origins in the comparatively dim and distant past and were brought in to cover circumstances disclosed by particular cases. They have hardly ever been used since and it has long been apparent that the code is crying out for modernization. Indeed, it is arguable that a service like the police force ought to have done away with such an archaic set of rules long ago. A strong body of service opinion favours abolishing the Discipline Code and treating all alleged misdeeds by policemen as 'unprofessional conduct', in much the same way as the professions discipline their members. Certainly there is an odd contrast here between the idea of the police constable, said by the Royal Commission on the Police to be unique among subordinates in his powers and responsibilities to the public, and a discipline framework which enumerates every possible minor infraction of accepted standards of conduct. 'You don't need a discipline regulation to deal with a scruffy policeman,' said a Lancashire constable. 'If he comes on duty with dirty shoes or no creases in his trousers, his sergeant should give him a rocket. As often as not, his mates will tell him to smarten himself up. It's no good charging him with an offence like that because it can only humiliate him.'

The elements of a disciplinary offence may be present in thousands of ordinary incidents which occur every day. Sergeants and other supervisory officers are expected to resort to the procedure only after everything else, including the 'word of caution or admonition' has been tried. The eight hundred cases which resulted in a formal charge and hearing in 1969 represented a comparatively small proportion of these matters, because the procedure allows wide discretion to deputy chief constables, who are responsible for deciding whether charges should be brought. All disciplinary invest-igations begin with the receipt, either from a supervisory officer or a member of the public, of the original complaint. If the deputy chief constable (who acts on behalf of the chief constable in the preliminary stages because the latter may have to hear the subsequent charges) decides that the facts alleged appear to be a breach of discipline, he must appoint an investigating officer, who is normally a superintendent who is not a direct superior of the officer involved. If it appears that the complaint is of a serious nature and likely to affect the reputation of the force, it is open to the chief constable to ask a senior officer from another force to take charge of the investigation. This happened on fifty-eight occasions in 1969 and throughout 1970 a full-scale inquiry into allegations of bribery made by *The Times* against two London detectives was conducted by an inspector of constabulary. The Home Secretary can order a chief officer to appoint an outside investigator, but has never found it necessary to do so.

The investigating officer is required, as soon as possible, to serve the officer involved with a notice setting out the nature of the complaint, informing him that an investigation is being held and inviting him to volunteer a statement under caution. It is the investigating officer's job to secure all the available facts, not merely to build up a case against the officer. When he has interviewed the witnesses and the officer, the investigating officer submits his report to the deputy chief constable, who decides whether formal charges shall be brought. If the complaint came originally from a member of the public the chief constable, unless he is satisfied that no criminal offence has been disclosed, must submit the report to the Director of Public Prosecutions, who decides whether the officer shall be prosecuted in court. In practice, nearly every such report goes to the Director. Out of 1,169 such 'criminal' complaints made to the Metropolitan Police in 1969, only six were not forwarded. It should be noted that the Director's decision that an officer shall not be prosecuted does not rule out any subsequent proceedings for disciplinary offences arising out of the incident complained of.

The investigating officer has one of the most thankless tasks in the service. He is well aware that he is serving two conflicting interests. He must be fair to the accused policeman and knows that any suggestion of pressing a case unduly will affect morale in the force and not improve his own standing with his colleagues. Against this, it is his responsibility to ensure that his investigation is honest and thorough, particularly when a complaint from the public is involved. At any time, his report can be scrutinized by either the Director of Public Prosecutions or the Home Office. Critics of the internal investigation system suggest that these inquiries are open to abuse. An interesting example of just how thorough they can be was the much publicized affair at Stockport. Three police officers were sued for assaulting pickets who had been arrested during an industrial dispute. Without admitting full liability, the Police Authority agreed to settle the case before trial but, as the plaintiffs were minors, the settlement had to be approved in open court. Here it was revealed by counsel for the plaintiffs that an investigation under the complaints procedure had been carried out by a senior officer of the Liverpool police who had recommended, in his report to the Director of Public Prosecutions, that there was a *prima facie* case of assault against the three officers. The Director decided, however, that criminal proceedings should not be brought. In court, the plaintiffs' counsel paid tribute to the fairness and thoroughness of the police investigation. One can only speculate on opinion in the Cheshire force about the investigating officer concerned, for the industrial dispute in question had been a long and bitter one and force feelings were running high, especially as in another incident at the factory an officer had broken his neck. Yet it had been the duty of the investigating officer to put such considerations of force morale on one side and report the facts as he saw them.

This case was interesting for another reason. Although the Director had decreed that the policemen should not be charged with any criminal offences, the Police Authority had agreed to pay compensation to the individuals who claimed that they had been assaulted while in police custody. Why, demanded the *News of the World* and others, were these 'guilty men' allowed to continue in the force and why had they not been disciplined by the chief constable? The obvious answer was that the only possible charges against them would have been of assaulting members of the public or prisoners. Yet, on the same evidence, the wholly independent Director of Public Prosecutions had said that no criminal charge must be brought. What the *News of the World*, some local MPs and others were demanding, apparently, was that these policemen should be punished by a police discipline tribunal on evidence which the Director of Public Prosecutions had deemed insufficient to put before a criminal court. Here was an interesting example of the standards of justice which some feel can be applied to the police.

Criminal or civil proceedings naturally take precedence over disciplinary matters, and where this happens an officer can sometimes find himself facing charges at a disciplinary hearing months after the alleged offence was committed. An obvious danger for an accused policeman is that a complainant will await the outcome of disciplinary proceedings before bringing a civil action for, say, assault or trespass. If a complainant indicates that he is proceeding through the courts, the disciplinary hearing will be postponed until the civil action has been disposed of, but there is nothing to compel a complainant to opt either for disciplinary or civil action, and he can if he wishes decide to take action after a disciplinary tribunal has found the officer guilty. To policemen, this looks as if a complainant has two bites at the cherry and it would obviously be more just if a complainant had to make a decision between civil action and the disciplinary procedure.

For serious disciplinary offences, and almost without exception for criminal matters, a policeman is suspended from duty under the discipline regulations. A suspended policeman cannot exercise any of the powers of a constable, although he could give evidence in any court cases pending during his suspension. The effect of suspension is effectively to separate him from the police force and his colleagues, while the charges against him are investigated.

There can be no more embarrassing and nerve-wracking time for a policeman than a period of suspension. Until 1971, suspension imposed a harsh financial penalty because a policeman was reduced immediately to an allowance of two-thirds of his basic pay, and forfeited certain allowances and opportunities to earn money through overtime. In

London, the result was that a suspended officer could be existing on half pay. He is not able to resign from the force while under suspension, unless permission is granted, and cannot obtain other employment. When it is realized that sometimes, as in the case of the officers involved in *The Times* bribery allegations, suspension can last for more than a year, it is not hard to imagine the mental stresses placed upon a suspended officer and his family.

One policeman was suspended pending a criminal charge and, months later, was cleared. He felt so incensed by the treatment he had received from some colleagues that he wrote a letter to the *Police Review*, thanking the true friends who had not treated him as a leper, and reminding others that 'a smile' sometimes meant a great deal.

A little humanity has been brought into the picture by allowing a suspended officer to remain on full pay during the period, but by its very nature suspension can only be a time of humiliation for the officer and distress for his family. Chief officers are well aware of this and every effort is made to complete an investigation quickly, but as it is only in the serious cases that suspension is used and these normally require long investigations, the problem remains a difficult one.

If, after considering the report of the investigating officer, the deputy chief constable decides that charges should be brought, the officer is served with a discipline form which sets out the charge and exact details including time, date and place. He also receives copies of all statements made to the investigating officer, but is denied access to the investigating officer's report. This is done on the grounds that such a report may contain matters concerning other officers which are not relevant to the proceedings.

The accused officer must be given reasonable time to decide whether he admits or denies the charge, and to prepare his defence. He can ask the chief officer to arrange for witnesses to be called on his behalf but he is not obliged to furnish their statements. Although legal representation is not permitted, he can have the assistance of any officer of any rank, who need not be a member of the same force. Often the 'friend' will be brought in from another force in cases where the accused officer is denying the charge and attacking the evidence of other officers.

The hearing is presided over by the chief constable, unless he decides that another chief officer should be asked to hear the case, either because he himself is somehow involved or because he has too great a knowledge of the case.

If an officer is found guilty of a disciplinary offence, he can be punished in a variety of ways. In 1969, for instance, officers in provincial forces who were found guilty were dealt with in the following ways:

Caution	96	
Reprimand	123	
Fine	218	
Reduction in pay	34	
Reduction in rank	13	
Requirement to resign	20	
Dismissal	59	(including 53 dismissed after criminal conviction)

A caution ranks as a finding of guilt but is not entered on an officer's record sheet, whereas a reprimand is so entered. Minor monetary punishments were imposed in more than a third of the cases. A reduction in pay means that an officer is dropped back in the incremental scale for his rank for a period, and a fine or fines must not exceed a total of thirteen days' pay, to be recovered in weekly amounts.

The major punishments are: reduction in rank, where the chief officer decides that the guilty officer is no longer fit to hold his position; requirement to resign as an alternative to being dismissed; and dismissal. Exactly one seventh of the provincial officers found guilty in 1969 were removed from the force by dismissal in this way. As such a punishment can entail loss of employment and accumulated pension rights, the consequences for such an officer can amount to thousands of pounds, to say nothing of the permanent stigma attached to dismissal from the force. It is just as well, therefore, that policemen can appeal to the Secretary of State against all findings of guilt. This is another innovation of the Police Act 1964. Previously, appeals to the Secretary of State could be made only in the cases where the most serious punishments had been inflicted. The chief officers at one time opposed a general right of appeal because, they said, too many frivolous appeals would be made. This has proved to be false expectation. Fifty officers appealed in 1969 and, of twenty-five appeals decided by the end of that year, four were allowed and the punishment reduced in eight others. Appeals are usually decided on the basis of the transcript of the hearing, but occasionally the Home Secretary will appoint a tribunal to conduct a fresh hearing. This happened once in 1969.

It can be seen, therefore, that police discipline is a comprehensive and sophisticated business, but need it be so? One is struck by the comparative mildness of the majority of punishments, and the near triviality of some of the charges—being late for duty, failing to submit an accident report and omitting to amend a copy of force orders all figures in the charges brought in 1969. Used for offences like these, the procedure becomes the sledgehammer cracking the tiny nut. 'Police discipline is supposed to be self-discipline among grown men,' said a West Country constable who had been fined for a minor infringement of force orders, 'so why keep a cane in the cupboard?'

In 1971 the chief constable of Dorset was severely criticized in the press for his action in fining several officers involved in the 'jackpot' incident, where a gambling machine in a police club paid out twenty pounds instead of the customary five. What annoyed so many people was the fact that the case had, for some reason, been reported to the Director of Public Prosecutions, who ruled that no criminal charges should be brought. Yet, on the same facts, the men were punished under the Discipline Code. Technically, the chief constable may have been correct, for not many police officers would argue that the men were entitled to keep money they knew had been paid out by the machine in error, but the impression was given that the chief constable was determined to punish them in spite of the Director's advice. Perhaps press comment was heightened by the fact that this chief constable has quite often figured in somewhat controversial cases involving discipline and management in the force. The *Daily Express* went so far as to ask whether he was fitted for the job.

But perhaps the most controversial aspect of police discipline is the widely different interpretations placed on what is, and what is not, 'discreditable conduct'. Some years ago, two young married constables in a northern force worked together in the CID. At about the same time, they both began to have affairs with women. One went with a single policewoman, the other with a civilian employee in the police station. Both were warned about their association. The detective and the policewoman resigned from the force, the other man went to London with his girl and joined the Metropolitan Police. He rose to a very senior position, and the force was not at all interested in the fact that he was living with a woman not his wife. Had he stayed in that small borough force, he would certainly have been disciplined under the discreditable conduct clause.

'A lot depends on the circumstances and just where the man is serving,' said a senior officer. 'It's easy enough to insist that it has nothing to do with the force. In a large city like London this may be true, but you can't have a married policeman going around with another woman in a small place where everyone knows him. That would be assuming that people are more broad-minded than they really are. They don't expect such behaviour from a policeman. It may sound a bit puritanical to take such a view, but policemen are expected to set a moral standard.'

Whatever its relevance to modern concepts of man-management in the police service, the discipline procedure must be retained in respect of complaints from the public.

Even so, the investigation procedures laid down in the Police Act seem to have produced a cynical reaction in some quarters. The Metropolitan Police has a special tie (not, one hastens to add, sponsored by authority) for members who have been served with Form 153 (Complaints). Some police officers say quite frankly that complaints do not worry them. 'If some joker comes into the nick to complain about me,' said a London detective, 'I won't lose any sleep. It just means I've been doing my job. I know I'm straight, so why should I worry. If it's my word against his. I expect them to take my word every time. If it ever happens the other way. I'll put my ticket in.'

Internal disciplinary charges can be a different proposition. Here there is no question of the bonds of service fellowship supporting the policeman in difficulties. A policeman who was charged with several offences against the Discipline Code, all relatively minor matters such as failing to keep station records properly and making a false statement to a senior officer (more an evasion of pending trouble than a deliberate lie) told me, 'I got the feeling that every man's hand was against me. They seemed to be making a mountain out of a molehill. I told the super who gave me the discipline form that it seemed a pity no one had anything better to do than chase a PC from one end of the station to the other. He said that he would tell the deputy chief what I'd said, and if I wasn't careful there'd be another charge of insurbordination.'

Even on comparatively small matters, any hint of disciplinary proceedings is sufficient to cause many policemen untold distress. Too often they are kept in suspense waiting for decisions to be taken, and it is little wonder that many people who are close to this problem feel that the police disciplinary procedure is crying out for a completely fresh and enlightened reappraisal.

Apart from any question of discipline and complaints, the police service in Britain attaches great importance to good relations with the public. This goes much further than pious declarations of intent from chief officers. Correct behaviour towards the public is a consistent theme of police training, and it is a measure of how seriously the police take their own responsibilities in this direction that the arrangements for dealing with complaints, for all the criticisms they attract, are more elaborate than anything which exists abroad. Indeed, the British police are probably unique in having legislation which specifically provides for complaints.

The police themselves are convinced that far too much attention is paid to their alleged failings and too little to their virtues. Their personal courage is taken for granted. The public expects its policemen to be brave, whether takling armed criminals or saving lives. The British take great pride in the image of the friendly, unarmed bobby and rarely bother about the great risks he faces. One of the reasons why police morale plunged so low in the late sixties was the equanimity with which Parliament overrode police objections to the permanent abolition of the death penalty, which policemen rightly or wrongly regarded as the greatest deterrent to armed attacks upon themselves.

Every year a number of policemen are decorated for gallantry, sometimes in incidents with criminals, sometimes for rescuing people from burning buildings or from drowning. The public notes, and takes satisfaction from, reports such as these, but the cumulative effect appears to be less than the shock of being told that police in Sheffield once used a rhino-whip to make prisoners talk. Most policemen learn to be philosophic about the public's often ambivalent approach to the service. 'These things go in cycles,' said a London inspector. 'After Grosvenor Square in 1968, or when the three lads were shot at Shepherd's Bush, we were everyone's friends. Just one bad case of bribery or corruption, and the public starts sneering again.' Perhaps the most startling example of the mercurial nature of police-public feeling was the Podola case, in which Detective Sergeant Purdy was murdered. An immediate response was the launching of a fund for Purdy's widow and children, but when Podola was caught, and photographs showed him with a black eye, the public mood changed abruptly. It was taken for granted that irate policemen had beaten up the police killer. There were questions in the House and demands for a public inquiry. Even the official explanation, that the detectives had charged a locked door with such force that it had come off its hinges and flattened Podola beneath it, attracted only cynical smiles. Police critics were disconcerted when Podola's own counsel went out of his way to state that there was no suggestion of police violence in the case. One lawyer said at the time, 'Of course he had to say that. No point in getting the jury's back up by making allegations against the police. After all, they were trying Podola for killing a policeman.'

When the public, largely because of press and television interest in a case, appears to be concerned about police conduct, the usual reaction of the service is to retreat behind its own defences. The police are not very skilful at putting their side of an argument. Sometimes, to be fair, the fact that criminal charges may be pending inhibits them from comment, but respect for the law and matters *sub judice* seems to be carried too far.

Television programmes come in for more police criticism than newspaper comment. The policeman is uncomfortably aware of the presence of television cameras at potential flash-points such as demonstrations. 'The police might have been on duty at a demonstration for hours,' said a London senior officer. 'Then you have just one flare-up as one small group gets out of hand. A few helmets roll in a scuffle, and a couple of demonstrators get dragged to a police van. It makes good television, just right for the introduction to the news bulletin, but it gives a totally false picture of what has been going on. We know for a fact that television cameras and their spot-lights egg a crowd on.'

At least in their relations with the press, the police appear to be doing better than they used to. Many forces have appointed public- and press-relations officers. Sometimes reporters complain that far from stimulating the flow of information to the press, these officers have been more interested in suppressing it. They say that their previous informal relations with the police, based on personal friendships with senior policemen, particularly detectives, used to work much better, but that nowadays such officers are reluctant to say anything. The press bureau at Scotland Yard, which is controlled through the public-relations officer, although some journalists have been added to its staff, is frequently criticized by frustrated reporters. The problem here is that newspapers are concerned with news, the police with detecting crime and catching criminals. Sometimes, there is a clear conflict of interest. The Metropolitan Police have often been criticized for their action in the case of Neville Heath, the sadistic killer of two women in the 1940s. They declined to allow the press to publish a photograph of Heath when he was wanted for the first killing and it is still maintained that publication would have saved the second woman's life. Yet the police knew that identification was likely to be a crucial issue in the trial, and witnesses would have been discredited if Heath's picture had been published. The case is a classic example of the opposing interest of the police and the press.

'I've had bitter complaints from newspaper reporters about names and addresses of people who are witnesses,' said a chief superintendent in a southern force. 'My view is that the police should not be the means of sending a reporter to knock on someone's door, especially if it's a personal case. It's not part of our job to help newspapers to write stories.' To which reporters would retort that the police are quick enough to seek assistance when they think the press can help. This is true, with many forces having the benefit of crime prevention columns in local papers.

'I find that the local press is always more reliable than Fleet Street,' said a Lancashire inspector. 'We get the London boys up here for big cases, or their Manchester staff. They are frantic to get information quickly, and preferably before another paper gets it, and naturally they aren't too particular about it. Some national reporters would think nothing of knocking on the parent's door in a child murder case, whilst the local reporter wouldn't dare go near. He's got to work with us after the big case has been forgotten, but the national man couldn't care twopence about local relationships.'

One inevitable consequence of the process of divorcing the police forces from local authority control is a certain loss of identity between the police and the communities they serve. Larger police forces inevitably mean more bureaucracy, with tighter control at headquarters and less delegation to local commanders. In this situation, the support of the local press for the police becomes additionally important.

But public relations with the police are much more than a matter of creating a shining brand image through the press. There is a fundamental need for a close rapport with all sections of the community, and particularly with that great mass of the public which belongs to no organization and takes no interest in civic matters. These people can never be reached by friendly chats to Rotary Clubs and Townswomen's Guilds. Yet it is their opinion of their local police which counts so much in the final analysis.

'The acid test of what the public thinks about you,' said a northern constable, 'is in a rough-house. If the public sees a copper on the ground and a mob putting the boot in, do they pretend they haven't seen anything, or do they go to help the copper? Are they ready to help the police because they know the police help them?'

8 Corruption

The reputation of the British police service has been built upon the integrity of its members, their respect for individual liberty, and their efficiency. Of these qualities, integrity is the most important. The law safeguards the citizen against abuses of police powers. Police efficiency is determined by professional competence and the degree of public support and co-operation that the service receives. Integrity is something that depends entirely upon the police themselves.

A policeman is in a unique position if he wishes to commit a crime. So much of his work is performed alone and his knowledge of police procedures gives him a huge advantage over the ordinary criminal both in opportunity and ability to evade detection. Occasionally (and the word needs to be stressed) a policeman betrays his trust. Seventy-eight were convicted of criminal offences in England and Wales in 1969 and the figures for other recent years are more or less constant. Of course, the total relates only to those who were caught; there is no way of measuring the full extent of police criminality. There will always be 'bent' policemen, just as there will always be lawyers who steal from clients and teachers who indecently assault their charges. A police service made up of ordinary human beings placed in situations where it is so easy to commit crime and faced with many temptations is bound to have some members who are weak and some who are worse than that. What matters in any consideration of police corruption is the ability and willingness of the overwhelming mass of honest policemen to expose the others. Because the British public accepts that the police service will deal with the few criminals in its midst, as and when they are caught, the general reputation of the police remains high.

This belief in the overall honesty of the police, together with the acknowledgement that not all policemen are perfect, was illustrated in the public-relations survey conducted for the Royal Commission on the Police. Although a big majority of the people interviewed admired the police as a body, as many as eight out of every ten thought that, occasionally, the police took bribes. This was not based on their personal knowledge, merely a general belief that these things happen and that this is a world in which every man is supposed to have his price. Some commentators at that time drew attention to the apparent anomaly between the survey's general conclusion that the public respected the police, and their willingness to believe that they could be bribed. A more likely explanation is that modern morality is such that people are no longer shocked when a delinquent policeman is exposed. If asked whether they believed that local councillors or civil servants took bribes, probably they would have answered 'Yes'.

Bribery of a police officer can take several forms. At its pettiest and most innocent it is the tip given by a grateful householder to the beat man who has kept an eye on his house in his absence, or the café owner who wouldn't dream of charging a policeman for a cup of coffee. This is harmless in itself, but many senior policemen frown on it because of what can follow thereafter. A very small borough force, which has since been amalgamated, was commanded for many years by a chief constable who had the technique of 'something for nothing' reduced to a fine art. It was said in the town that he never paid the retail price for anything. Not surprisingly, some of his senior officers followed his example. The first action of the new chief constable was to rid the force of the men he could not trust, then he set about the local traders who had curried favour with the police and made it clear that henceforth everything obtained by a policeman would be paid for in full.

The idea of 'police perks' is sometimes deeply rooted in local communities. Traders think that offering discounts to policemen is a natural way of maintaining good relations. 'This has died out a lot recently,' said a sergeant in a Lancashire town, 'but it still happens. I remember when if we wanted to hire a car we went to a local firm and got it for next to nothing. Now we all have our own cars. Or we could go to some shops and get things like furniture for practically wholesale price, but now there's no need, for nearly everyone gives a discount for cash, or you can buy from a discount firm.

Police 'perks' become less innocent when such things as free pints in public houses are considered. The police have heavy responsibilities for licensing, and a policeman who has accepted a landlord's hospitality is not in a good position to act impartially when offences come to light. Some forces have had to take disciplinary action against police car crews who have had cosy arrangements with local garages by which they have cornered the accident market. A garage which stands to make a big profit from repairs would be happy to pay a small gratuity to a constable who called them to the scene of an accident. Now most forces insist that all local garages have an equal share of accident work.

None of this, however, is the kind of serious corruption which undermines police integrity. Those who told the Royal Commission's survey team that they thought some policemen took bribes were thinking of more serious incidents, such as those in which a policeman takes money to 'forget all about it', or worse still, accepts part of a criminal's takings to leave him free. Policemen have been convicted of bribery in such cases in recent years, but the statistics do not give the precise number of cases. It needs to be said that allegations of bribery are made much more often than they are proved, and often they are made with deliberate malice against a particular policeman whom the criminal wants to discredit. The Kray brothers were known to have tried this tactic against a London policeman who was making life difficult for them.

A policeman may be disciplined even after being cleared in court. 'We must ignore the fact that there has been a criminal charge when a man is being disciplined,' said a senior officer, 'but sometimes this is almost impossible. It is not that a discipline hearing requires less proof of guilt than a court, but it is entitled to draw certain conclusions from a course of conduct which is against our rules. For instance, a man may be charged with not entering details of, say, a valuable watch in a found-property book at the police station. But, if the watch is missing it is reasonable to assume that he stole it.'

It sometimes happens that the mere fact that a policeman has at some time been involved in a corruption allegation, even if no action has been taken against him, can have a ruinous effect on his career. 'A prostitute once complained that I had stolen five pounds from her handbag,' said a sergeant. 'It was a lie from start to finish, but I always had the feeling that they believed her and not me. I kept being passed over for promotion then one day I got a chance to look at my own personal file. They keep them under lock and key but this time I saw it and sure enough, there it was. It was just a memorandum about me and promotion. It said I was an efficient policeman and a hard worker and then, "Unfortunately, this sergeant does not enjoy the complete confidence of his superiors." What could I do? I couldn't admit that I'd seen the file or they'd have put me on a charge for that.'

For obvious reasons, the extent of bribery in the police force is impossible to assess. Only the rare cases come to light. To read some criminal memoirs, one would gather that a large proportion of the CID is amenable to bribery. The commonest allegation is that a policeman has been 'sweetened' with money to persuade him not to oppose an application for bail, or not to say too much in court that would damage a prisoner's chance of getting a light sentence. Suggestions of this kind are often made in letters of complaint to the Home Office by men in prison who feel that the detective in their case has let them down.

'The detective is obviously in the best position to take a bribe if he wants to,' said an experienced senior detective. 'He's close to the criminal, and often he alone knows enough to put a man inside. So the punter comes along with an offer and sometimes, just sometimes, it works. But ninety-nine times out of a hundred it doesn't. No one ever tried to bribe me. They would have been inside before they could say Jack Robinson. You'll hear a lot of stupid talk by thieves about how they fixed so-and-so, but it's nearly always just bragging.'

What is remarkable about so many of the reported cases in which policemen have been accused of bribery in the courts is the paltry sums involved. In 1970 two policemen went through three trials (two juries having failed to agree) before being acquitted of trying to get twenty pounds from a man accused of fraud. When it comes to bribery on the grand scale one has to go far back in police history to discover a policeman who made a fortune by taking bribes.

Station-sergeant George Goddard stands alone in the category of the corrupt policeman. He was the officer whose activities in Mayfair shocked the country in the 1920s. Goddard was in charge of a small squad which was detailed to supervise the night-clubs, legal and otherwise, which flourished in the West End after the First World War. Prior to this, George Goddard had been in charge of another squad which was supposed to suppress street betting. In 1922 a young sergeant called Josling arrested a bookmaker and was warned by Goddard to leave the betting boys alone. If he did, said Goddard, he 'would see him all right'. Josling was a man of high principles who thought it his duty to report Goddard to his superiors. Instead of investigating Goddard, however, the senior officers promptly charged Josling with making false statements about him. Josling was sacked, and seven years were to pass before the Home Secretary admitted that a miscarriage of justice had taken place.

This escape made Goddard feel that he could do no wrong.

When transferred to club work, he made thousands from his rake-off from the takings of several clubs. When he was caught, the police found over £12,000 in one safe deposit box at Selfridges, and there were rumours that this was just one hiding place for his profits. He operated during the Empire Exhibition at Wembley, although in court he admitted that some of it came from bribes from bookmakers. Goddard and two of his accomplices in the night-clubs were convicted at the Old Bailey. Mr Justice Avory gave him a remarkably lenient sentence of eighteen months hard labour and a heavy fine. On his release, Goddard was able to sue for the return of the money from the safe deposit, and won the case. The judge, in sentencing Goddard, had not followed the advice of prosecuting counsel and dealt with him under the Prevention of Corruption Act, which would have meant a sentence of seven years penal servitude. Perhaps the judge agreed with the general view that a man of such low rank could not have continued in this way for so long without support from higher up.

For its sheer effrontery and vast scope, the Goddard scandal remains the worst in police history. That he was a villain is clear enough (although I have always been struck when talking about Goddard to policemen of those days that they admired him for keeping his mouth closed about his colleagues), but not enough attention was paid at the time to the factors which had encouraged him. Goddard was operating in two fields which were wide open to police corruption. If all London night-clubs had operated in strict compliance with the licensing and gambling laws of that time, they would have closed their doors at once. The street bookmakers flourished because the law was held in general contempt. Yet it was another thirty years before the law was changed, and petty corruption continued more or less undetected in the years that followed the Goddard case. This much was admitted when it was stated that the Gaming Act of 1960 would remove one of the obvious avenues of corruption. The same could be said of the Street Offences

Act. Before it was passed, it was often alleged that the police took bribes from prostitutes and operated an unofficial 'rota' system by which street-walkers, like bookmakers, were arrested in their turn and bailed immediately to return to their beats.

It says something for the general reputation of the British police that when one of them is exposed as corrupt the case still causes surprise and is given publicity. In America, it is only when corruption is on the grand scale, spreading throughout an entire force, that anyone seems to be shocked. A few years ago, Chicago discovered that much of the serious crime in the city was being committed, planned, or connived at by policemen. In 1970, Mayor Lindsay of New York announced a far-reaching inquiry into police corruption and appeared on television to ask the citizens to tell him what they knew. There has never been the slightest reason to suspect that a British police force has become so riddled with corruption that no member of the force could be trusted.

Perhaps this was why the Brighton conspiracy case created such a stir in 1957. It had all the ingredients guaranteed to cause a sensation: a chief constable and two of his detectives arrested and kept in custody; lurid stories of police blackmail and a night-club called The Bucket of Blood, all set in the town with a household, if wildly inaccurate, reputation for naughty weekends. The press made the most of the story, and the overall impression that was given was of a police force working hand in glove with the local criminal fraternity. The case had resulted from the suspicions of policemen from outside Brighton that they were being hindered in their investigations into a crime by the activities of some Brighton officers. After a trial at the Old Bailey, a detective inspector was gaoled for five years and a detective sergeant for three. The chief constable was found not guilty. Sentencing the detectives, the judge said that he took into account the fact that they had not received from the chief constable the kind of leadership one expected from a man in his position.

The Brighton case had repercussions. The chief constable, the late Charles Ridge, had spent almost his entire career in this one small force and it was obvious that he had become too close to certain elements in the town. It was after the Brighton case that the Home Office began to insist that in future chief constables should have experience in other forces. For the men who remained, the task of living down the notoriety of the case was a hard one. An inspector at that time, who has since retired from the force, told me: 'It was bad in the town. Your friends tried to be sympathetic, so they never mentioned work to you. The smart-alec types made cracks and even my wife had to put up with remarks in shops, things like that. What hurt most was the attitude of the new bosses. Those of us who'd been promoted under Ridge were made to feel suspect in some way, as if we must have been tarred with the same brush. The new chief was a disciplinarian. He was a good policeman but he came with instructions to "clean up Brighton". There wasn't really anything to be cleaned up, but everyone felt the pressure.' When, in 1971, it was announced that nine young constables in Brighton (now part of the Sussex constabulary) had been suspended and charged with theft, the thoughts of many policemen would have gone back immediately to the events of 1957.

Few forces have suffered so much in this direction as the Leeds City Police. In just over two years, eleven members of the force have been convicted of criminal offences ranging from theft to indecent assault on children. The culmination was the conviction of two officers for conspiring to pervert the course of justice. In this case an inspector and a sergeant were sent to prison for what amounted to an attempt to 'cover up' the truth about a fatal accident in which a car driven by a superintendent in the force had knocked down an old woman on a pedestrian crossing. Two constables had attended the scene, but the inquiry was promptly taken over by the sergeant and the inspector. The constable claimed that they had suggested that the superintendent ought to have been given a breathalyser test (it was Christmas Eve) but had been told it was unnecessary. It was also said that afterwards the sergeant had said to the constables, 'It's a poor job if you can't help a colleague'. A lying story was told at the inquest about the position of the woman at the time she was knocked down and the two constables alleged that strenuous efforts were made by their superiors to make them change their accident report. A good deal of dirty linen was washed at the trial, with one defendant suggesting that a police witness who could help his case was afraid to come forward. Counsel said that one department of the force had been seething with rumour about the case. In the same trial, another inspector and a superintendent were cleared.

The case came to light because the two constables, after the inquest, had gone to the coroner to tell him what they knew. After all that had taken place inside the force, they felt unable to confide in their superior officers. This was in many ways the most disturbing feature of the case. The trial judge must have realized the situation in which these officers found themselves. At the trial he said, 'Plainly they showed great moral courage over a long period in very distasteful circumstances. They could not have enjoyed for one moment their involvement in such matters.' Some press reports suggested after the case that the constables were being ostracized by some members of the force.

The two constables were faced with an agonizing conflict of loyalties. When the sergeant and inspector were convicted the judge said, 'It is plainly of paramount importance that the police force in this city, as elsewhere, should be beyond suspicion, and that justice should be administered impartially without fear or favour.' This was stating no more than the obvious, yet the actions of the two men which led them to prison were based on an immediate and instinctive desire to help one of their own. If they had caught another colleague in the act of breaking into a shop, in all probability they would have done their duty immediately. In these circumstances, it seemed natural that they should try to get him out of trouble.

Soon after the Leeds inspector and sergeant were convicted, another and even worse scandal was revealed, involving the same inspector, Geoffrey Elleker. Gossip within the force about the first case led to a young cadet hearing of some rumours about the death of a Nigerian vagrant, David Oluwale, whose body had been recovered from a canal. Elleker, already dismissed from the force, was charged with manslaughter. A similar charge was made against a serving sergeant, Kenneth Kitching. Other charges alleged that they had hounded and harassed Oluwale, and had assaulted him before he died.

At the trial, the Judge intervened to direct the jury to dismiss the manslaughter allegation. He said that there was no evidence before the court as to how Oluwale had met his death, and no one could be convicted on suspicion and rumour. Elleker was found guilty of four charges of assault on Oluwale and jailed for three years; Kitching received twenty-seven months for three charges of assault. The jury's verdict meant that they were satisfied that Oluwale had indeed been brutally treated by these two officers. Again, the trial revealed a disturbing situation in that officers gave evidence for the prosecution, alleging that Elleker and Kitching had assaulted Oluwale in their presence, yet none of them had made any complaint until the matter had been reported to the chief constable many months after Oluwale's death. It was suggested that this was either because the officers concerned lacked confidence in the ability of superior officers to deal with such matters in a proper manner, or because it had taken an inquiry into the matter to force witnesses to reveal what they knew. The defence suggested that some of the police officers were lying because of their personal dislike of Elleker and Kitching. Because Elleker was already under a cloud when the inquiry started, he was 'a sitting target for a purge', suggested his defence counsel.

Oluwale was said to be a mental defective and a man who

was so filthy in his habits and so aggressive that he could not be helped by any of the social agencies. Prosecuting counsel told the jury that it was true that Oluwale had not complained about ill treatment, but asked, 'What chance do you think Oluwale would have had that any complaint he made would receive sympathetic consideration or anxious investigation?'

The outcome of the trial led, inevitably, to demands that the Home Secretary should appoint an inquiry into the Leeds force. After receiving a deputation of local MPs, he decided to ask the Chief Inspector of Constabulary to conduct a special inspection of the force. This fell a long way short of what the Members of Parliament had asked for, and it should be noted that the Home Office Inspectorate in such a case can hardly be regarded as a disinterested party. The Inspectors of Constabulary are responsible to the Home Secretary for the efficient administration of the police forces. If there was anything seriously wrong with the Leeds force, they ought to have known about it. Again, the terms of reference of the Inspection were not disclosed in public. If it resolved itself into an inquiry into what had occurred at the police station involved in the Oluwale case, the officers who gave evidence at the trial would be making statements to a police official. In all the circumstances, the Home Secretary seemed anxious to avoid any further public exposure of the force and to guard against the danger of a public witch hunt; whether he had averted the danger of a private witch hunt was another matter.

The Judge in the Oluwale case referred, in passing sentence, to the fact that the verdict 'added fuel to the fires of those who spend their time sneering at police officers and making brash criticisms of the police'. He might have added that the case had damaged confidence in the police among other citizens who could certainly not be classed in this way. The situation was not helped, either, by the news that several other Leeds officers were due to appear in court on criminal charges following the Oluwale case. As it happened, these were cases in which persons who had themsleves been charged had brought cross-summonses against the police. When the first of these cases was heard, the police officers concerned in it were cleared.

That the Leeds police could expect a great deal of adverse publicity because of all the cases mentioned above was inevitable. If anything, what they got was worse than this: for months after the trial, any mention of Leeds policemen was good for a laugh on television or in the press.

'Knocking off a copper for thieving is one thing,' said a London constable, 'booking him for speeding is another. If you stop a driver and he tells you he's in the job, what do you do? You ought to report him like anyone else, but nine times out of ten you'll let him go if you can. No one wants to look a right bastard to another copper. But when it comes to crime, I wouldn't stop to think about it. He's not a copper any more, he's just a thief.'

Some police critics would claim that this loyalty to colleagues extends to protecting policemen who assault prisoners or perjure themselves to gain convictions. 'There's nothing like as much verballing* goes on nowadays as it did when I was starting in the job,' said a London detective. 'If a prisoner said to me now, "It's a fair cop, guv," I wouldn't put it in my book. Everyone would think I was making it up. It's what you used to say just to clinch the case. Nowadays, they're nearly all defended on the taxpayer and they ask to go for trial. Then it doesn't matter how much they coughed in the cells, they'll deny every word of it in court and you finish up being the one that's on trial.'

'We had two brothers in this force twenty years ago,' said a Lancashire policeman in a former borough, 'everyone thought they were the best policemen in the north of England. I mean that. They were respected by other forces and the thieves were scared to death of them. Some of the stories I've heard about them make your hair stand on end these days. Like how they'd get to know when a villian was

---

*'verballing' — putting damaging admissions in prisoners' alleged replies.

due out of prison and within a few hours of getting back here he'd be inside, because they'd found him in possession of stolen property. What had happened was that they'd have given him the chance to have that job taken into consideration when he was sent down. If he wouldn't have it, and they knew he'd done it, well they'd just arrest him for it when he came out. Unscrupulous if you like, but it was during the war when there were too many real hard cases around. It was their way of keeping down crime. Try it today and they wouldn't last five minutes. It's everything by the book today. It's safer, but it doesn't let us catch thieves.'

The readiness of members of the public, and particularly juries, to believe that the police beat up prisoners to extract confessions, is strongly resented by many policemen. 'We brought in a bloke who runs a doss-house, for interfering with kids,' said a Lancashire inspector. 'It was a bad case and the kids were too young to give evidence. He wouldn't have it at first but we got it out of him and he made a statement. Then in court he went back on every word of it. His barrister just said to me, "How tall are you, officer? How much do you weigh? And how big was your colleague?" Then he turns round to look at this little chap in the dock. In other words, two great hulking brutes bullying this poor little bloke. The jury found him not guilty in ten minutes.'

Almost daily in the criminal courts a defence counsel attacks police evidence, alleging that an officer is lying. To many young policemen, giving evidence can be an ordeal. The older officer has learned to cope with the wily lawyer.

'I was giving evidence at Assizes in a burglary case,' said a northern detective. 'It was the first time I'd been there and really I was just corroborating a detective sergeant. I'd been with him to arrest the prisoner and was there when he interviewed him. The defence barrister demanded to see my pocket book, and asked me all kinds of questions about it. This force is very strict on entries, and I'd made a couple of mistakes. One was a time, I was about five minutes different from what the sergeant had put. And I'd got some words out of sequence in one of the prisoner's replies. Now I knew I'd made a mistake and had altered a couple of words. Not to cook anything, just to get the facts right. But this barrister went on about it as if I'd been made to alter the entry by the sergeant, And the judge asked for the book and studied it. Then he asked me if I realised how serious it was to alter pocket-book entries like that. I came out of court feeling as if I'd lost the case and my job as well. Lucky for me the jury found him guilty after all.'

Police witnesses are vulnerable when counsel probe, in minute detail, their actions at the time when a suspect is interrogated and arrested. The Judges' Rules, a set of instructions laid down at the beginning of this century and revised a few years ago, are specific as to the limits of police questioning of persons in custody. They state that once a police officer has made up his mind to charge a suspect with a crime, he must first caution him. The caution tells an accused person that he is not obliged to say anything and that whatever he says may be given in evidence. Once a man has been charged and cautioned, he must not be questioned further about the offence mentioned in the charge.

If defence counsel is confronted with a prosecution case that relies heavily upon incriminating statements made by his client, inevitably he will try to establish that these were obtained in contravention of the Judges' Rules. It will be put to the officer in the case that he delayed charging the man beyond the point when he had made up his mind to arrest him, simply to be able to go on interrogating him until an admission was made. Or it will be said that the questioning went on for hours, without a break for refreshments, or that he was prevented from contacting his solicitor, or that the police promised him that it would be in his interest to admit the offence. The whole tenor of the cross examination will be aimed at establishing a picture of hulking policemen giving the third degree to a frightened suspect.

So many criminal trials turn into a battle of wits between defence counsel and police witnesses that often a jury finds itself trying, not so much the question of guilt or innocence of the accused, but the honesty of the police. This situation has had an understandable effect on the police attitude towards lawyers.

A Lancashire detective said: 'We had a case where a man was charged with housebreaking. His house was piled high with stolen gear. We'd spent months trying to catch him, special patrols, the lot. Then when we got to sessions we lost the case because his lawyer made a fool of a very young detective. It was awful. That young copper got down from the witness-box looking as if he was going to be sick. I couldn't say anything to make him feel better. He just thought he'd ruined everything and his CID career was over. Then this bloody lawyer came up in the corridor and said, 'No hard feelings, officer, it's all part of the game.' I thought the constable was going to hit him. He grabbed his shoulder and shouted, 'It might be a bloody game to you, but it's not to me.' Well, the lawyer reported him straight away. They asked me what had happened and I just said I hadn't seen anything wrong.'

Lawyers would insist that their first duty is to their client. The police would not resent vigorous cross examination if they had nothing to hide and, say the lawyers, they should remember that sometimes policemen have been known to lie on oath, to bend the Judges' Rules, even to plant evidence and frame innocent men. A High Court judge wrote some years ago that when such cases occurred, it was not because a policeman was evil, but because his sense of righteous indignation against crime (and a legal system weighted heavily in favour of the accused) tempted him to break the rules to achieve justice as he saw it.

Inevitably, when this question is discussed, the name of Harold Challenor, formerly a detective sergeant at West End Central police station, comes to mind. For some police critics, and for some who are sympathetic to the police but concerned about the implications of such cases, Challenor is the embodiment of all the dangers inherent in a policeman who allows his desire for justice to become an obsession.

Challenor's police career ended in 1964 when he was invalided out of the service on medical grounds (with an ill-health pension) while three young men, inexperienced constables who were hoping one day to be detectives, were beginning long prison sentences for what they did, acting under his orders. The contrast between what happened to Challenor and the severe punishment of his subordinates is not the least unhappy feature of the whole case. When everything had been revealed, Challenor stood exposed as a policeman who had appointed himself as a one-man instrument of society's vengeance against the criminal, a lone crusader who believed that the end justified the means. The Metropolitan Police, in so far as the conduct of senior officers and colleagues of Challenor was concerned, came out of the proceedings with a big question mark over their standards of supervision and their ability to act immediately when grave doubts about Challenor had arisen. Although it is fair to say that the judicial inquiry exonerated the force from active complicity in what Challenor had done, this did little to allay public misgivings at the time.

Challenor's early history is almost a standard description of the background of so many police recruits. Born in 1922, he left school at fourteen and spent his youth as a motor mechanic, a male nurse and a lorry driver until he joined the army. He was dropped behind enemy lines in Italy to blow up trains, was twice captured and escaped. When Company Quartermaster Sergeant Harry Challenor, MM, was demobbed in 1947, he worked as an iron-moulder until, in 1951, he joined the Metropolitan Police. Normally, the force is not over anxious to accept men who are so close to the maximum age limit for recruits (then 30) unless they have special qualifications. But Harry Challenor was a good recruit, the kind of man who could be expected to make a first-class policeman. He had knocked around a bit, gaining a valuable experience of life outside the force. He had proved his personal bravery. He was a happy extrovert, perhaps a little undisciplined, but (as an early report put it) Harry Challenor was 'a police officer with a tremendous appetite for work, a good-natured man with a good sense of humour, noisy and a bit of a rough diamond.' Someone at the police training centre must have congratulated himself some ten years later for the percipience which made him report on Challenor the recruit: 'He seeks diligently after knowledge and at times needs someone to keep a brake on his excess of energy.'

From the start of his police career, there was only one thing that Harry Challenor wanted, to become a detective. So, for that matter, do thousands of other young policemen. There has always been keen competition for the CID. But Challenor was not an ordinary young policeman. His obvious interest in crime was clear from his first days on the beat. When still in his first two years of probation, he was taken off the beat to become an 'Aid' to CID. At that time, this was the recognized way of entry into the detective branch. Young officers selected for this work were not full members of the department. They were not paid the usual detective allowances but worked in plain clothes. A surprising number of the arrests made by Aids in those days was for the offence of 'being a suspected person loitering with intent to commit a felony'. It was a relatively simple charge to make. Two Aids would testify that they saw the prisoner loitering near parked motor cars, or in similar circumstances, in a suspicious manner. Often this would be a perfectly correct charge, but the frequency of such arrests in the Metropolitan Police district used to raise some police eyebrows in other forces.

As an Aid, Harry Challenor was an unqualified success. In nine months he amassed the astonishing total of 105 arrests for crime. He was efficient and enthusiastic, yet still he had to wait another two years before being sent to the Metropolitan detective training school at Hendon, preparatory to being accepted as a fully fledged detective. Subsequent reports on Challenor after Hendon, where he was a star pupil, used up all the usual superlatives. He was 'excellent', a 'magnificent worker', he was continuing to 'forge ahead'.

Indeed he was. By 1958, Harry was appointed to the elite 'Flying Squad' and within a month it was reported that he had already made his presence felt, even in such exalted company, by his 'initiative and drive'. Harry was revelling in the pursuit of the major criminals with whom the Flying Squad was constantly at war.

It was Challenor's superior officer in the Squad who first submitted a report that went somewhat counter to the high praise of all the other assessments. Chief Inspector Butler did not care for Challenor's manner, which he described as 'brusque, blunt and boisterous'. Butler agreed that Challenor was a very good policeman, but he was 'inclined to noisy tactlessness'. Perhaps the truth was that Harry at this stage was rather out of his element. Senior officers of the Flying Squad and others in the Scotland Yard hierarchy were unused to being addressed in the familiar way that Harry Challenor spoke to everyone, regardless of status. He had a habit of calling people 'me old darling'. So, when he was promoted to second-class detective sergeant in March 1962, Commander Hatherill, commanding the CID at that time, decided that he should be posted to a station away from the West End. This was because it was thought that he would do better in a working-class district than in Mayfair. But a few months later Harry was back in the West End, working in Soho and attached to West End Central police station, perhaps the busiest police precinct in Britain.

Here began Harry Challenor's incredible war against the thieves and villains with which that small part of London is populated. His new chief, Detective Superintendent Townsend, was even more pleased with Harry than his other superiors had been. He reported that Challenor was 'working very hard' and had 'developed a knowledge of the problems of the division well in advance of many longer-service officers.' In other words, Harry was getting spectacular results and certainly the criminal fraternity knew that they had a deadly enemy in their midst.

By this time, Challenor had been commended for outstanding police work on eighteen occasions. He was so well thought of that he was one of the two detective sergeants at West End Central who were responsible for the training and discipline of all the Aids attached to the CID there. This meant that young constables who, like the Harry Challenor of a year or two earlier, had a burning ambition to be detectives looked to him for the advice and assistance they needed. He was a hard taskmaster and a disciplinarian. These young men knew that their future in the department depended almost entirely on what Challenor said about them. This man, who thought nothing about working twelve hours and more a day, every day of the week, expected the same dedication from the Aids. He had no time for clock-watchers. At the same time, he could be encouraging to the keen youngster, and the Aids often approached him with their personal problems. In many of them, Harry Challenor inspired a fierce loyalty. It was a case of there being nothing that Harry would not do to help a good colleague and, as it turned out, nothing that they would not do to help him.

In spite of working such long hours over a continuous period, Harry still found time to study and pass his promotion examinations. He was promoted to first-class detective sergeant in July 1963; ironically at just the same time that the first serious doubts about him were being voiced at Scotland Yard.

In April 1963, Challenor and another detective sergeant were put in charge of a special squad with orders to work only at night and check the rising crime rate in the area. Within four weeks, the Squad had to be discontinued, not because it was a failure, but because it was successful. The number of arrests made during the night meant that the members of the squad were spending their mornings, when they should have been sleeping, in court. There was an obvious limit to the amount of work that a man could perform in a week, even if Harry Challenor seemed to defy all the laws of nature in this respect.

It was Challenor's exceptional hours of duty that, at this

time, began to worry Detective Superintendent Townsend. He was quite obviously working too hard, he look exhausted, and he was having trouble with his hearing. Mr Townsend advised Harry to ease off, but the detective sergeant insisted that he was getting on top of the Soho thieves, he did not want to lose his grasp. In this answer to Detective Superintendent Townsend, Challenor should have set the warning bells jangling. Here was a policeman who was convinced that he, and he alone, was cleaning up Soho, and he was determined that nothing should stop him. Far from taking Mr Townsend's advice, Challenor if anything worked longer and harder. In a five weeks' period in the early summer of 1963, his recorded hours of duty were: 76, 88, 80¼, 91 and 102. Commander Hatherill was to testify at the official inquiry which examined all aspects of the Challenor case that such hours were 'a bit too heavy'. Incredibly, the other detective sergeant in the special squad managed to work even longer hours in this period.

Mr Townsend had another reason, beside Challenor's health, for being concerned about this officer. Challenor had made such an impact in Soho that the criminals had begun to hit back through the usual complaints technique. As Mr Townsend told the inquiry: 'If a man is doing a job of work and is being continually complained about, then as a senior police officer, one has to take notice of the position and try to take him away from the scene until the position has been clarified.' Two men had complained that Challenor had planted detonators on them. Four men arrested by Challenor and other officers at a club said that they had been planted with offensive weapons. A solicitor's clerk complained about Challenor's conduct when he tried to interview a client at a police station.

So the position in 1963 was that Harry Challenor was hard at work in Soho, attacking the thieves, ponces and petty racketeers who infest the district. His superiors in the force were delighted with his results but worried about his health and, perhaps, beginning to have doubts about his methods.

Then, on the night of the 11 July 1963, came the incident that
led to the end of Challenor's police career and one of the
worst scandals in police history. The Queen was due to be
entertained at Claridge's Hotel by the King and Queen of
Greece, whose visit to Britain had aroused strong opposition
from left-wing circles. The police knew that there would be a
hostile crowd of demonstrators outside Claridge's and drafted
every available man to the area. Challenor's squad was
detailed for this duty. He and his Aids arrested a young
anarchist called Rooum and six other young people during
the course of the evening. All were charged with possessing
offensive weapons – pieces of brick. Challenor and his
subordinates claimed that they found the pieces of brick in
the pockets of their prisoners. They all denied it and insisted
that the half-bricks had been planted on them. Rooum
realized that he was being planted and acted with remarkable
presence of mind. He chose to remain in custody overnight,
and refused to sign for a list of his property that contained
mention of the half-brick. This was done in order that he
could have the pocket in which Challenor claimed to have
found the brick scientifically examined. He had to establish
that he had not had an opportunity to tamper with the
evidence after being released from custody.˙The test was
made by arrangement with Rooum's solicitor the following
day and this evidence helped to create a doubt in the
magistrate's mind when the case was tried a month later. In
the course of the case against Rooum, the defence established
that three pieces of brick, said to have been found on three
separate prisoners, came from the same whole brick.

When Rooum was acquitted, the full realization of what
Challenor had been up to had still not dawned on the
authorities. Yet the sergeant's whole pattern of conduct
during the Claridge's affair had been extraordinary. When the
prisoners were charged at the police station, Challenor had an
argument with the duty inspector. A superintendent who
intervened and ordered Challenor to 'pull himself together'
told the subsequent inquiry that he was incoherent, shouting,

shaking, and waving his arms about. The superintendent thought at first that the man was drunk, then wondered if he was on the verge of a nervous breakdown. Mr Townsend also rebuked Challenor at the station for shouting at him. The inquiry concluded that allegations that Challenor assaulted his prisoners that night were true, saying that the assaults were committed 'in the excited and emotional state which was a symptom of the mental illness then affecting Detective Sergeant Challenor, but not diagnosed until later.'

Whatever was thought by his superiors about Challenor's conduct that night, the fact remains that the prisoners, all of whom denied their guilt, were charged on his evidence and that of his subordinates, the young Aids.

Rooum was determined to have justice. He issued a writ against Challenor alleging false imprisonment. (He and others received compensation in an out-of-court settlement.) When Challenor was waiting with a chief inspector for this writ to be served on him by appointment, he said, 'I'm a simple man and I know what I'm paid for but I'm just not being allowed to do my job.' When he attempted to leave the station before the writ was served, the chief inspector became alarmed and took him before a chief superintendent, to whom Challenor, by this time in an agitated state, said, 'These villains are doing their best to crucify me.'

More complaints were coming in about Challenor. Rooum's solicitor was one source, another came from a Member of Parliament acting on behalf of one of the boys in the half-bricks case. A further allegation was that Challenor had assaulted a coloured prisoner on a criminal charge.

In September 1963, the chief medical officer again examined Challenor, and this time he had full details of various odd incidents in which Challenor had been involved. Challenor was returned unfit for police duty. A month later, whilst attending a CID dinner, he broke down completely and was admitted to a mental hospital.

It was not merely the half-bricks case which was concerning the National Council for Civil Liberties and some half dozen Members of Parliament of all parties who were pressing Henry Brooke, the Home Secretary, to hold an inquiry. The NCCL claimed that Challenor had charged twenty-six innocent men, thirteen of whom were in prison at the time of the half-bricks case.

Yet it took another ten months before Brooke rose in the House of Commons to announce that he was recommending free pardons for five men charged by Challenor and referring another five cases to the Court of Criminal Appeal. Three of the pardons concerned youths who had been convicted of carrying half-bricks at Claridge's. Two men who had been gaoled for conspiracy and possessing offensive weapons were granted free pardons (one had completed his sentence).

There was an immediate public outcry. The public inquiry appointed by Brooke in August 1964 was asked to examine the circumstances in which it was possible for Challenor to have been on duty at a time when he appeared to have been affected by mental illness. The inquiry reported that Challenor's illness was of such a nature that it would not have been possible to diagnose it earlier, that Challenor's superiors had acted correctly in putting the sergeant before the medical officer, who was not in possession of all the facts about him on the first two occasions that Challenor was examined. It is only fair to add that the tribunal rejected any suggestion that other officers (apart from the three young PCs who were already in prison) were involved in Challenor's saga of trumped-up charges. Indeed, reading the full report* leads one to wonder why free pardons were granted in some cases. The tribunal found that there was not the slightest ground for suggesting that Challenor had solicited or accepted bribes, as some witnesses had alleged.

Challenor and three young constables who had worked under him as Aids were charged with conspiracy to pervert the course of justice in relation to the half-bricks case. Challenor was found unfit to plead. The constables were

*Report of inquiry by A.E. James, QC (*Cmnd. 2735*), HMSO, 1965.

convicted. Two were sent to prison for three years, and one for four (reduced on appeal to three). Mr Justice Lawton listened to what their counsel had to say: that Challenor was their immediate commander, that he was something of a tyrant, but that he was highly thought of at the time and if they had complained about his behaviour it would only have been their word against his. His Lordship was unimpressed. He had told the jury: 'There comes a time when police officers, just as army officers, just as anybody else, when they are told to do something which is clearly wrong, have to say to those in authority above them, " I can't do it. I won't do it." It is no answer for them to say, "I had orders from Challenor to do what I did".'

Passing sentence, the judge said: 'Honest police officers are the buttress of society. But dishonest, perjured officers are like an infernal machine ticking away to the destruction of us all. As intelligent young men you must appreciate that a crime of this gravity must be punished, and the punishment must be such to show the revulsion of this court at your conduct and to warn any other police officer who might be misguided enough to do what you did of the dangers he is running.'

The young constables had no real answer. As at Nuremburg, so at the Old Bailey. A policeman cannot say, 'I was only obeying the orders of my superior.' But the contrast between the treatment meted out to the underlings and to the prime mover in this affair still reeks of injustice. What those young men did was criminal, and unforgivable. Yet would they have done anything of the sort if they were acting under their own volition? And did Mr Justice Lawton really believe that they could have gone to their superiors and reported Challenor for trying to frame his prisoners? Harry Challenor, that 'wonderful copper' as so many of his former colleagues still describe him? Three young men wanting to make their careers in the CID? One wonders what consolation they received from the knowledge that their police careers were ruined while Challenor, thanks to his insanity, never went on trial and to this day receives a police pension.

Challenor is important, not so much because of what he actually did, though that was bad enough, but because of what he represents. Here was a truly remarkable man, and this description is applied without malice. Harry Challenor knew that his mission in life, as a policeman, was to catch thieves. Indeed, it was only when he was quite suddenly and almost accidentally taken out of his element and confronted with a young and articulate anarchist with a nimble mind that he was finally destroyed. Within his character there must have been a distinctly puritan streak that took one look at the Soho scene and was outraged. Here were the dregs of criminal society, living off crime in a state of near-immunity from the law, because the police were powerless to catch them by normal methods. What Challenor did was throw all the rules of the game overboard. He went up against the thieves, 'felt their collars', and made sure that his evidence fitted the charges he brought. He was supremely confident, perhaps because he was indeed suffering from paranoid schizophrenia, as the medical evidence stated. Perhaps he saw himself as the embodiment of honest society against the criminal parasites. And, as arrest followed arrest, and conviction piled upon conviction, so his confidence grew. How else could be explained such an astonishing incident as that in which Challenor, who was giving evidence against five men he had arrested in a Soho club on another 'offensive weapons' charge, arrested four men in the precincts of the magistrate's court, originally for using 'insulting words and behaviour', and succeeded in getting them committed for trial charged with conspiring to pervert the course of justice by the intimidation of witnesses? Two of the men were deaf mutes. Probably they were acquaintances of the five men whom Challenor had already arrested. The inquiry found that this arrest was unjustified and further evidence of Challenor's mental illness.

Public reaction to the Challenor case ranged from the shocked surprise of the pro-police middle classes, expressed in Mr Justice Lawton's scathing condemnation of the convicted constables, to strident left-wing suggestions that Challenor was but the tip of a giant iceberg.

Mary Grigg's book, *The Challenor Case* (London 1964) posed a whole series of pointed questions. She wrote: 'Could one man have created such a situation? Could a second-class detective sergeant, with a flair for inventing crimes and composing prisoners' statements, outwit his colleagues, his superior officers and the courts, day by day, for a period of more than a year?' Dealing with the issues raised by the case, and with the type of investigation that she thought should have been made, Miss Grigg wrote: 'One would have to discover why no one inside the police force ever reported Challenor's activities, why none of the young officers in his charge felt able to speak to a superior officer about what was happening. Was it because they were afraid? Or was it because they had no way of judging whether or not Challenor's behaviour was normal for a police sergeant?'

The Tribunal, in its report, gave its own answer.

I have given [wrote Mr A.E. James, QC] particular consideration to a possible additional factor which was urged upon me as a cause of Detective Sergeant Challenor remaining on duty when mentally sick. The factor is a subtle and indefinable one which can best be described in this way. In any disciplined force there are rules and regulations which must be observed. Nevertheless in order to get on with the job in hand there is always the temptation to disregard a rule, 'to take a short cut', or to subscribe to the view that the end justifies the means of getting there. An atmosphere can grow which, if allowed to grow, undermines discipline and produces wrongful acts and omissions. It is the atmosphere in which the lower ranks of a disciplined force know that there are certain things which are contrary to regulations and which are wrong, but they also know that they are allowed to do those things provided that they are not found out, and no one is going to try very hard to find out. It was submitted to me, with tact and moderation which enhanced the force of the submission, that at West End Central such an atmosphere had developed whereby police officers, and Detective Sergeant Challenor in particular, could use violence and show disrespect to persons in custody, and could indulge in the fabrication of evidence without exciting attention.

Mr James reported that he had reached the conclusion that the evidence put before him did not support this suggestion. Indeed, the whole of the available police evidence to the Tribunal had tended to show that, during the period when Challenor was pursuing his war against Soho crime, senior officers were showing a proper concern about his state of health. That this never for one moment appeared to give rise to doubts about some of the charges he was making was not Mr James's concern. He had not been appointed to decide on how much of the responsibility for a series of mis-trials and false arrests devolved upon others. His terms of reference began with the assumption that Challenor was mad, had been mad for months, and as such ought not to have been in a position where he was capable of wreaking such havoc.

But the issue raised by the Challenor case was nothing less than the corporate integrity of the British police. Challenor could operate, mad as he was, and secure convictions against people he believed to be guilty of some crime (and I am convinced that he did so believe) because he belonged to a police force which had established for itself the right to be believed. Challenor's colleagues and his predecessors had earned that right over many years. The tendency of the criminal courts to take a policeman's word in preference to a prisoner's is based on a simple belief that policemen do not lie. But Challenor lied, and three other policemen were found to have lied with him. Did this case, involving so many miscarriages of justice and so many other cases where a miscarriage might have occurred (the Appeals Court quashed the convictions which had been referred to it by the Home Secretary) point to a police force which had become so obsessed with catching criminals that it believed the ends justified the means? Was it true that the police, while not hesitating to expose a colleague who was a thief or a bribe-taker, would protect a colleague who had perjured himself and bent the rules to put criminals away?

These were the questions begged by the Challenor case. They defied a complete answer because there was no way of discovering the whole truth. Challenor was unique in the sense that there was no parallel case in police history. But, after Challenor, it became very much easier for the police to be criticized in court and in Parliament and for their honesty to be questioned. This was the measure of the external damage. What of the harm done within the force? In one sense, the mental illness which protected Challenor at his trial was highly convenient for the police. It was possible to attribute all the happenings to this source and to seek comfort in the thought that nothing of the kind would have happened if Challenor had been sane. It was a case of Challenor having a split mind and his underlings having split loyalties. His superiors were exonerated because they could hardly have been expected to diagnose mental illness.

Policemen had every sympathy for Harry Challenor, and for the three young men who had gone to prison. There was a tendency to attribute Challenor's actions to the strain of months of overwork. Indeed, the Police Federation said at the time that the case pointed to the urgent need to reduce the excessive hours of the CID and to bring their caseload within acceptable limits. There was some official action in this direction, but in 1971 the average hours worked by detectives in the Metropolitan Police were over 70 a week.

The police, and particularly the CID, are operating against a constantly mounting crime total; the number of indictable offences has doubled in ten years, with almost two out of every three remaining unsolved. It would be stretching credibility to insist that no police officer would deliberately lie to improve the chances of convicting a prisoner when the pressures and frustrations are so high. What critics of the police prefer to ignore, however, is the chain of supervision which provides a check against excesses. Police forces operate under strict rules of procedure and these invariably require the detective to keep meticulous records of his daily activities so that he can be supervised as far as is consistent with the nature of his duties. Many an unfortunate detective has found himself in trouble because he has failed to carry out standard procedures during an investigation.

It is, of course, quite impossible to provide for every conceivable situation which can arise in a criminal invest-igation. Indeed, the idea of detectives operating strictly according to some kind of manual of criminal investigation is faintly ludicrous. It is by his individual flair and initiative, often his unorthodoxy, that a policeman becomes a good detective. But he must face the consequences if that very individuality lands him in serious trouble when an invest-igation puts his every action under a microscope.

No detective can succeed by holding himself aloof from criminals. They are his stock in trade. He has to know them and establish some kind of relationship with them, even though all the time he has to walk a tight-rope between the permissible and the irregular.

'Nearly every good arrest comes through an informer,' said a Manchester detective. 'When you've no other evidence, it's only the tip-off from someone that tells you who to look for. A good detective looks after his regular informants. He does them little favours, like turning a blind eye if they've done something trivial or helping them to get bail when they've been arrested. I get as much information for the price of a drink as I do by using the informants fund, only because I've always played straight with them. You don't have to like a thief and you don't have to make a bosom pal of him. But a good informant is worth his weight in gold.'

It is because detectives are obliged to mix with criminals that there is an ever-present danger of a policeman stepping across the thin and vaguely defined dividing line between correct conduct and the discreditable. 'I worked with a detective sergeant who was returned to uniform because it was said that he was too familiar with convicted thieves,' said a London detective. 'They had a full-scale inquiry on him, watching him all the time, and there were plenty of thieves ready to put the poison in. Because I worked with him, I was under suspicion as well. They did him for about half a dozen petty little things like neglect of duty, the sort of thing every CID man forgets to do every day of the week. If he hadn't been close to a pension he'd have jacked it in. But all the time the force was losing a bloody good detective just because someone upstairs didn't trust him.'

The public controversy which arose in 1969 over the manner in which detectives in a number of different forces were alleged to have 'set up' crimes in order to trap criminals revealed the sharp contrast between what the criminal courts, and especially Her Majesty's judges, and the working detectives regarded as ethical conduct.

The 'set-up' can have many different circumstances, but broadly speaking it is a case in which the police, either on their own initiative or by encouraging an informer to act as an *agent provocateur*, persuade a known thief to take part in a robbery, then lie in wait to catch him in the act. In these cases, it is sometimes essential to allow the informant who is betraying his accomplices to take part in the crime, then allow him to 'escape' before he can be arrested. In 1969, the Court of Criminal Appeal threw out a conviction after it had been established, largely because of an exposure in a Sunday newspaper, that a robbery on a post office had been a classic 'set-up'. The judges declared, in an angry condemnation of the police, that by not revealing the facts at the trial they had made certain that 'justice was blindfolded'.

Similar moral indignation against such tactics was behind the disciplining of several officers at Preston, shortly after the case mentioned above. Here too it was said that an informer had been permitted to escape. The result was that the Home Office sent to all chief constables a stern warning against the use of an *agent provocateur* in such cases, and instructing the police to act with scrupulous care in cases where they received prior information about a projected crime. Many policemen were indignant at the apparent hypocrisy they detected in the Home Office attitude.

'Sometimes the only way you'll ever catch some criminals is to be on the job when they get there,' said a London detective. 'It's OK if we get a straightforward tip that a warehouse is going to be screwed. All we do then is wait all night getting frozen to death and if we're lucky and the information's right, we're on. I wish I had a fiver for every night I've wasted on one of those. The really worthwhile tip off is the one that comes from the bloke that's in on it, and knows the time, date and place, how many in the mob, everything. To know all that, if it's a big one like a wages job, he's not just on the fringe, listening to careless talk in a pub, he's one of them, with a job to do, like driving the car or breaking the doors open. The Home Office says we mustn't let him go ahead with it. If he doesn't, the job's off. If he does, he's supposed to be nicked. But if he backs out he can be in dead trouble with the hard boys, because straightaway they know he's been grassing. Christ almighty, it's a dirty game, but it's only one side that knows the rules.'

Policemen appreciate the difference between 'acting on information received' and what is sometimes alleged about the 'set-up', that there was no crime in the offing until they put the idea into an informant's mind. 'It takes some doing when you stop to think about it,' said another London officer. 'Look what it means. Say you know that a certain thief is living off crime and committing offences all the time. He's got to be caught, and he's too smart to be caught on a job or even with the gear. Right, the next thing is to go to someone else, maybe an informant or someone who'll do it for money, and set up a place to be screwed. First you've got to be sure that the bloke you've chosen is good enough to act convincing and then you've got to be sure that the other bloke's fallen for it. Then everything's got to work like clockwork until he's neatly locked up. It sounds all right, you just try it. And if it's got to be a whole team to be set up, it's almost impossible. I can't see it working very often'.

Whatever sympathy might be felt inside the police for colleagues who have been convicted of perjury and similar offences because of an excess of zeal in their attempts to catch criminals, there is none at all for the policeman who turns thief. That an occasional policeman steals on his beat, or even breaks into a house, is not surprising. The mere fact that a man is a policeman does not put him beyond temptation. What is baffling is that some recent episodes have involved groups of policemen working together to commit crime. The recent Brighton case was an example of this, with young constables stealing from cars and property. A similar instance occurred in Croydon a few months earlier and in the last three years there have been several other cases. It would be a gross exaggeration to describe this as a trend, but one senior officer confessed that he was worried. 'The only real safeguard against a crooked policeman is the honesty of all his colleagues,' he said. 'I have always believed that a policeman would not hesitate to arrest a colleague, even a close friend, if he caught him stealing. But these cases proved the opposite. Are we getting a different type of young man in the job, or is it because constables on the beat are not properly supervised?'

This officer's point was that nowadays individual policemen work on their own initiative and their activities cannot be watched as closely as they used to be, when men patrolled fixed areas on foot and supervising officers were expected to visit them on their beats. This certainly increases the opportunity for a policeman to commit a crime if he wishes to, but does not explain why policemen should act in concert.

Society can take comfort in the knowledge that a crooked policeman is still newsworthy. There is still a deep sense of shock in the local community when a case is revealed, simply because the overall reputation of the force stands so high. 'The real time to start worrying about corruption and crime in this job,' said a detective superintendent, 'is when no policemen are in the dock. So long as they are arrested and punished, there's nothing wrong with the whole body.'

9 Crime

Every now and again, the state of crime in Britain becomes a matter of public concern. The great train robbery showed how efficient and successful the well-organized and ruthless gangs have become. People were horrified by the slaughter of three policemen in a London street in broad daylight. The moors murders case revolted public opinion and brought demands for the restoration of hanging. Yet public moods are volatile. It takes an outstanding crime to shock the ordinary citizen out of his usual complacency. Perhaps ten years ago a single bank raid with a haul of £10,000 would have attracted headlines, but now, when it is commonplace for a security guard to be coshed or even shot if he offers resistance, even the spectacularly lucrative crimes are forgotten within a day or two, except by the police investigators.

Politicians sometimes see votes in the law-and-order issue. At the 1970 General Election, strengthening the police and getting tough with criminals were major planks in the Conservative manifesto, with an implication that Labour was 'soft on crime'. In office, the Conservative Home Secretary, Reginald Maudling, redefined law and order as meaning 'justice under the law' and gave little sign of overturning his predecessors' policies. It is left to the police and other law enforcement agencies to be constantly concerned with crime. This, after all, is their principle function.

Ordinary policemen are not given to making broad statements about crime and criminals. Unlike the fictional characters of television, they do not go around professing a burning hatred of offenders. In fact, police feeling against criminals is in general confined to hatred of the types who would excite loathing in anyone: the child molesters and the violent thugs.

'There's too much talk about the big criminals,' one detective sergeant told me. 'They don't make up the crime figures. For every Kray or Richardson there's a thousand little blokes who live by knocking off what they can get their hands on. The country's full of petty thieves who keep going in and out of prison. They make the statistics go round.'

Many policemen disliked the former system of preventive detention under which habitual offenders could be given long sentences purely to keep them out of harm's way. 'PD was bloody unfair,' said one detective. 'It didn't touch the ones who ought to have been put inside for a long time. I've seen some poor old devils given eight years for petty larceny simply because they were the ones who were always getting caught. But the right bastards who did the break-ins and used violence would come up in front of the same judge and get probation.'

Sociologists write books on the causes of crime. The old belief that crime was caused by poverty has been shaken by the expansion of lawbreaking in an affluent society, but other current explanations are that crime stems from the frustration of the 'have-nots' within an acquisitive society, or from environmental problems associated with the deprivations of the inner city, or from young people's lack of a clear sense of direction from their elders and their failure to find a clear purpose in life, and so on. Policemen tend to be impatient with theorists. 'We're not concerned with the causes of crime, but with its effects,' said a chief constable. 'We are interested not in why a man committed a crime so much as whether he did in fact do it. It's our job to discover the authors of crime. Treatment or punishment is not a police concern.'

Not all officers would accept this detached view. 'We're always being told that it's our job to put people in front of the court. What happens to them is not supposed to concern us, but it does,' said a Lancashire constable. 'If we know that chummy has been living off crime for a long time and intends to go on living off crime, we want to see him locked up for a long time. If he gets put on probation or fined, it makes us wonder if it was worth the trouble of catching him.' The police view is that the only deterrents to crime are a strong police force to enhance the chances of detection, and stern punishment of the guilty. This is not due to a sense of vindictiveness against offenders, but to a belief that the courts have a duty to protect society from the criminal. In some ways, magisterial harshness is equated by the force with 'backing up the police'. Deterrent sentences, passed by the courts as an example to like-minded offenders, receive strong police approval.

Older policemen greatly admired the late Lord Chief Justice Goddard for what they regarded as his 'no-nonsense' approach to crime. Goddard and his contemporaries on the bench met the challenge of the first post-war crime 'wave' with maximum severity, making full use of their powers to order corporal punishment until flogging was abolished. ('They never came back for the "cat" a second time' is often quoted as fact by policemen of this generation.) Goddard has been hotly criticized for his handling of the trial in which Derek Bentley was condemned to death for the murder of a policeman, although the shot was fired by a juvenile, Craig, while Bentley was being arrested. To the police, Goddard's attitude to this case and the fact that Bentley was hanged gave him the reputation of being a judge who would back up the police to the limit.

'We could do with a few more like old Goddard today,' said a London inspector. 'They couldn't pull the wool over his eyes.'

Recent years have seen a succession of liberalizing measures in the criminal law. Nearly all have attracted hostility and suspicion from policemen. Suspended sentences are regarded as a failure because of the high incidence of further offences being committed during the period of suspension. Homosexual law reform was regarded by most policemen as indicative of the moral degeneration of the nation. The Labour Government's proposals for raising the age of criminal responsibility struck many policemen as idealism gone mad. Probation officers and juvenile court magistrates do not enjoy a high reputation with most policemen. 'I've listened to probation officers making all kinds of excuses for crime,' said a London detective. 'They get taken in too easily. You hear them in court saying how the prisoner's been trying to go straight and all the rest of it, and all the time the bloke's laughing up his sleeve at them.'

As to juvenile court magistrates, the police view of most is that they are well-meaning do-gooders with no real understanding of the depths of child criminality. 'It's no good lecturing the little sods,' said a Yorkshire sergeant. 'What they need is someone to put the fear of God into them. If young hooligans were sent to a detention centre every time they went out smashing other people's property, there wouldn't be any problem. Now they just get fined or told not to do it again. They're laughing at the law, and they come out of court laughing at the police.'

In police eyes, leniency shown by magistrates and judges is partly responsible for the steady increase in crime. 'You can look at a typical criminal record for a middle-aged habitual thief,' said a senior detective, 'and you'll find the usual pattern. It starts off with a few juvenile court appearances when he's been given an absolute discharge and probation. Then he's been sent to an approved school, then it's more fines and probation, then Borstal, then gaol. By the time he's forty he's spending as much time inside prison as he is out. Now, if we hadn't been soft the first time he went wrong, if he'd had a good hiding as a juvenile or the 'short shock' treatment at a detention centre early on, would it have been different?'

Enlightened penal methods have helped to put the police into a more isolated position. They find their generally conservative attitude to crime and punishment being undermined by legislation and the actions of judges and the Home

Office. The Parole Board, introduced in the middle sixties, is regarded by many policemen as a body which releases dangerous criminals on to the streets to commit further offences. Each well-publicized case in which a paroled prisoner commits a further crime is greeted as proof positive of the 'softness' of the Parole Board.

For the type of policeman who believes in retributive justice (and most policemen do) the passing in 1965 of the Silverman Act to abolish capital punishment for murder seemed like the last straw. The late Sidney Silverman incurred the dislike of the force because he was so often involved in criticism of police actions in individual cases. It was said by some policemen that Silverman was anti-police because his brother had served prison sentences for fraud. The truth was that Silverman's early experiences as a Liverpool solicitor in working-class areas had shown him a side of police nature, as it was in those days, that few ordinary citizens suspected. Whatever the reasons for Silverman's actions, or for the policeman's dislike of him, it seemed to be just one more added insult that he should be the politician who ended hanging. At the time of abolition, the police as a body believed that Parliament was taking from them the one effective protection against murder. When in less than two years following abolition, six policemen had been murdered compared with none in the corresponding period before the Act, it looked as if the police were right. Subsequent experience has been less disturbing and the fear that the abolition of hanging would lead to more murderous attacks on the police during the commission of crimes has been largely dispelled. Yet in 1969, when the Police Federation conference debated the question, the executive's mildly phrased proposal that the police should seek the reintroduction of hanging for the murder of a policeman or anyone going to his assistance, an amendment calling for hanging as the penalty for all murders was carried overwhelmingly.

The rise in violent crime over the past decade has left its mark, in one sense literally, on the policeman. Each year about eight thousand policemen and women are assaulted in the course of their duty. Some are so badly injured that they have to leave the force on a much reduced special pension, most of which is swallowed up by ordinary National Insurance benefits (which are deducted from police pensions). Others may not at the time be forced to retire through injury, but the after effects of the beatings they have received are such that in some cases they can no longer perform ordinary police duties in the streets, or their self-confidence has been destroyed. 'We used to have a station cleaner,' said a Lancashire constable. 'He had been a copper until one night a gang beat him up with his own truncheon. He'd been bright and full of guts. He used to shuffle around the station with his mop and bucket. We used to look at him and wonder if we'd finish up like that.'

In the days when a policeman's physique was his major asset, assaults could be dealt with in a more informal manner, but what was accepted then would not be permitted today. The police may use only enough force to restrain a violent prisoner, retaliation in kind is forbidden. So the police look to the courts, and here the common complaint is that the police are not protected by the magistrates. Some years ago, York magistrates dealt with a case in which a gang of at least twenty youths had attacked and kicked unconscious a lone policeman. Two youths were arrested and fined a trifling amount. The magistrates explained that as so many had been involved they thought the two who had been charged were unlucky. Less than a year later, the same young policeman was assaulted once again. This time he quit the force.

One chief constable told me: 'I got so sick of seeing my officers being attacked that I told the force photographer to take colour transparencies of their injuries before they had been treated. These were shown to the magistrates and at first they were so shocked that they started to send a few to prison. Then the magistrate's clerk asked me not to submit any more coloured pictures because they sometimes upset the lady magistrates and he was afraid that an appeal court might think that the magistrates had let their emotions influence them.'

'It's this spontaneous violence that makes you sick,' said a Leeds constable who had been badly assaulted at a football match. 'What can you do about someone who jabs a razor blade in your neck in the middle of a crowd and when you turn round there's no sign of him and no one's seen anything? A few years ago a football match was a nice pleasant way of earning a bob or two extra. You saw the crowd in and then you watched the match. There was never any trouble. Now your wife starts getting moody from the time you finish your dinner and she's a bag of nerves until you get home again.'

The growing number of police assaults prompted an interesting piece of research during 1971 by a senior officer attached to the Police College. He conducted a survey in three forces, two urban and one partly rural. The incidence of assaults, not surprisingly, was twice as high in the urban areas as it was in the rural force. The factors associated with violence were the attitude of offenders towards the police (in an area where the police are unpopular, respect for the uniform is no protection against attack); the ability of individual policemen to defend themselves; the level of police activity; drunkenness; and violent demonstrations.

One interesting point made in this study was that the level of police activity contributed towards the increase in assaults simply because police response to incidents was nowadays faster and more comprehensive. Whereas the policeman called to a fight outside a pub at closing time would once walk towards the scene, be seen to be approaching, and arrive at a point where tempers were beginning to cool, now the Panda car screeches to a halt and the constable jumps out to be embroiled in the fracas before he has had an opportunity to assess the situation. 'The immediate confrontation which results,' the senior officer concluded, 'is more likely to lead to violence against the police.'

The use of the motor car as an offensive weapon figured

prominently in the survey, with case after case in which a car was deliberately driven at an officer. This appears to be symptomatic of a trend which has been observed for some years now, that more and more motorists resort to violence in traffic incidents.

The main conclusion drawn from the survey was that the police needed more effective training in self-defence than the somewhat elementary instruction they have been given in the past. As a solution to the problem of assaults this may be effective, because the ability of the policeman to meet force with force would act as a deterrent, but the consequences for public relations could be disastrous. 'Reasonable force' by police officers can so easily be called brutality.

That violence is on the increase in society cannot be disputed and no one suggests that the trend can be ignored or minimized. In other areas of crime, opinion is not so unanimous. 'Statistics can mean anything,' said a superintendent. 'When you look at the hundreds of thousands of simple theft charges you could get the impression that the country's going to the dogs. We ought to be more concerned with how much crime is really serious, how much really threatens ordinary people.' Part of the explanation for soaring annual crime figures is the vastly improved system of recording crimes. At one time it was fashionable in the police for crime figures to be doctored to produce an artificially low overall total and misleading high detection rate. 'You can still get a sudden improvement in detection figures by getting one prisoner who'll have a big list of other offences taken into consideration. Every one counts as a detected crime and it makes your figures look good,' said a detective inspector. Nowadays, when police chiefs insist that crimes are recorded as such, and not written off on the pretext that they may not have been crimes (stolen property recorded as simply lost, etc.) the gap between the total of crimes committed and those detected grows larger despite the increase in detection rates in recent years.

The police have been turning their attention away from a

simple consideration of crime in terms of statistics towards a closer analysis of what the figures mean in terms of social damage to the community. In other words, which crimes are so serious that every effort must be made to prevent and detect them, and which are relatively trivial in the sense that they involve minor thefts where the only loser is the complainant? This revised attitude may be born of despair that the police will ever make serious inroads into total crime figures, but it is developing into a far more realistic appraisal of police priorities. If police manpower is such a precious resource, it follows that the best use of manpower in the fight against crime is that which concentrates on the dangerous offenders. This view is in accord with what society expects of its police. If the public worries about violence in the streets, well-planned armed robberies, attacks on children, and so on, it is for the police to demonstrate that they share this concern and have arranged their priorities accordingly. In 1969, following pioneer work in this field in America by two professors, Thorsten Sellin and M.E. Wolfgang,* the Home Office Police Research and Development Branch began its own studies of the feasibility of a crime-seriousness scale. Sellin and Wolfgang based their scale on a survey of attitudes to particular kinds of crime by a wide cross-section of citizens, including police officers, who were asked to assess the seriousness of a crime by having regard to its constituent elements of violence against the person, intimidation, methods used and value of stolen property. English criminal law has traditionally placed heavy emphasis on the sanctity of private property, a situation which in itself places the police, in the eyes of some sections of the community, as protectors of property and the property-owners. It would be reasonable to suggest that nowadays people would place more importance on the role of the police as protectors of the citizen against violent attack.

The advantage of having, at least in general terms, a scale

*The Measurement of Delinquency, John Wiley (New York, 1964).

of seriousness for crimes would be that police resources could be allocated to dealing with the types of crime that society as a whole finds unacceptable. If the police are to concentrate on violence, for example, such crimes as shoplifting and thefts of property from unattended motor cars, which account for a significant proportion of the total crime figures, would have to receive less attention. Among police officers the prevalence of both these types of offence causes some resentment because they are clearly preventable offences. Supermarkets appear to be unwilling to sacrifice profits in the interests of better security of goods, yet employ elaborate systems of television surveillance and hordes of store detectives to trap customers who yield to temptation. One former chief constable at Southend caused an uproar some years ago when he suggested that in future police would not prosecute shoplifters because of the social irresponsibility of the supermarket owners.

In other directions, police organization in recent years has reflected an awareness of the differing importance of various crimes. The formation of the regional crime squads was a natural development in the task of dealing with the greater mobility of the criminal and the squads are now expected to concentrate their efforts on the so-called 'target' criminals — men whose activities represent a threat to society.

The shortage of police has compelled chief officers to become more selective in their enforcement policies. Chief constables have to exercise their discretion as to which criminal offences require more police attention than others. Manpower considerations have also dictated an artificially low establishment for CID strengths, as chief officers have been reluctant to strengthen their detection resources at the inevitable expense of the preventive branch — the uniformed patrols. Herein lies the explanation for the enormous case-load borne by CID officers, a persistent problem which has defied a satisfactory solution for more than twenty years.

The size of the police task in combating crime, therefore, needs to be seen in terms of its social consequences rather than of sheer quantity. It is the clear-up rate for robbery and violence which is important, not the depressingly high total of simple thefts.

If the pattern of the 1960s is to be repeated in the future, the outlook is bleak. The fact that so many criminals use violence as a matter of course rather than as a last desperate resource has increased the hazards faced by the police and the ordinary citizen. Firearms are a particular anxiety at this time. Only a few years ago, the idea of an armed police force was so repugnant, not only to the public but to the police, that it was unthinkable. The police see a direct connection between the abolition of capital punishment and the significant rise in the instances where firearms have been used against the police and in the commission of crime.

'In the old days a man who carried a gun and killed someone was bound to be hanged,' said a detective superintendent. 'He was regarded as a nut case by other thieves and no self-respecting criminal would work with him. Now the sawn-off shotgun is standard equipment for a bank raid or an attack on a security van. They've got nothing to lose, because if they're caught they'll go away for at least ten years anyway, maybe a lot longer. It they shoot their way out, they stand a chance of escape and if they're done for murder, what's the difference?'

The great majority of policemen would still resist the notion of being armed as a matter of routine, but the service has had to come to terms with reality. Every force now trains a proportion of officers to handle weapons, and there is far less reluctance than was once the case to authorize the carrying of firearms on occasions when it is thought possible that criminals may be doing the same.

To the police, the fact that so much liberal legislation has changed the criminal law, at the same time as the rapid increase in violence has changed the nature of the crime situation, is seen as clear evidence that politicians have got their priorities wrong.

'No one seems to realize that we are fighting a war,' said a

London sergeant. 'We've got to stick to the rules when there are no rules at all for the other side. Unless people wake up to the truth, we're never going to win. And if we don't win, all I can say is God help the public.'

10 Immigrants

The recruitment of a coloured constable is still such a rare event that the occasion is bound to attract publicity, with press photograph of the recruit and hand-outs from the force's public-relations department. The police are eager to advertise their lack of colour prejudice and each new coloured recruit is looked upon as another example of their willingness to break down barriers.

Whatever the general state of the relationship between police and public, the police themselves are only too well aware of the unhappy nature of their dealing with Britain's immigrant community. They react strongly to the frequent allegations of colour prejudice made against them by such bodies as the National Council for Civil Liberties and the militant groups which claim to speak for immigrants. Much of the agitation for independent investigation of complaints against the police is linked with this situation. No matter how vehemently the police as a body deny discrimination, many people firmly believe that it is common practice for coloured people to be beaten up in police custody, to be made victims of police perjury and harassment in their homes and clubs, and to be planted with drugs.

The whole question of immigration assumed major political significance in the sixties, and as the pressures have mounted the police have found themselves too often at the eye of the storm. Now the question needs to be seen as a problem not so much of immigration as of the rapidly mounting numbers of young coloured people, all born in this country and ready to demand equality of treatment in all walks of life. Recent incidents in Notting Hill and North

London have involved friction between white police and coloured youths. It is a question which arouses strong feelings amongst the police, especially those who work in immigrant areas. In areas like Brixton and Notting Hill, pointless misunderstandings arise with lightning suddenness, leaving the police baffled and resentful. 'One of our cars on an emergency call was in a fatal accident,' said a Notting Hill inspector. 'It was a pure accident. He swerved, mounted the pavement and knocked down a coloured man. In two minutes flat there was a coloured crowd round the car, screaming for blood. If we hadn't got there quickly I don't know what would have happened to that driver.'

Policemen who have spent all their service in one area have a strong sense of community attachment. Those who live and work in areas which have built up high immigrant populations in a comparatively short time share the local resentment against the drastic changes which have taken place. 'I knew this district before the war,' said a sergeant in the Chapeltown district of Leeds. 'It used to be a very good neighbourhood. Then we got all these wogs and just look at it. Well, look for yourself.' We were driving through street after street of dilapidated mid-Victorian terraces. Immigrant children below school age played in the roadway, women in saries gossiped on front steps strewn with litter. Many houses had broken windows and the front gardens once tended with pride were mud patches. As it happened, I knew the district well from my early childhood. The sergeant, was correct in saying that it had once been a select neighbourhood, but its decline dated from a time long before the immigrants came to Leeds. The houses which had been built for families started to become flats for multiple occupation between the wars, housing the Jewish workers in the clothing factories. The first primary school I attended in the thirties had a roll in which Jewish children outnumbered gentiles six to one. Now it has children of many nationalities and no Jews. They have moved out to the prosperous suburban belt north of the city and the coloureds have moved in. A former synagogue is now a mosque.

Once the Jews were the immigrants. I was dimly aware, even as a small child, of the powerful anti-Semitism that existed below the surface. This rarely spilled over into violence, even when Mosley's fascists strutted on Woodhouse Moor or put up a racialist candidate in a pre-war by-election. The resentment against the Jews stemmed more from their financial success and control of so much local employment than from any other reason. Feelings against coloured immigrants are far more deep-rooted. The situation seemed to be getting out of hand in 1969 when mobs of 'Paki-bashers' started attacking immigrants, but the police acted swiftly to stop trouble. On this occasion, at least, there were few complaints about discrimination.

The frequency of clashes between the police and immi-grants has prompted some senior officers to make genuine efforts to improve relationships and it is common to find community liaison officers in forces with immigrant pop-ulations. So far, their efforts have not resulted in any significant improvement in the general situation. 'We honestly go out of our way to make contact,' said a senior police community liaison officer in London, 'but what can you do when the only articulate spokesmen they've got will say anything to get a headline?'

Many policemen admit that they dislike having any dealings at all with coloured people. 'You get a radio message to go to a disturbance,' said a Birmingham constable on motor patrol, 'you can tell from the address what you're going to find. If it is a a West Indian, and it nearly always is, you just don't know what to expect. It could be an assault, it might be a knife, but one thing's for certain, gaffer, it's going to be nasty. They just hate policemen. They take it in with their mother's milk.'

The frequency with which coloured prisoners make alle-gations against the police is the major reason why so many officers are apprehensive about dealing with them. In several reports and surveys on relations between immigrants and the police, attention is drawn to the number of allegations and the very small number which are said to be substantiated. Magistrates are criticized for preferring the police evidence to that of the coloured man. It is not only immigrants and organizations sympathetic to their problems which voice this concern. After a street riot in 1970 in Notting Hill, the *Kensington Post* mentioned some local officers 'whose names are known to almost every member of the coloured community' . . . who . . . 'were only to be involved in a charge against a coloured man for the innocence of that man to be assumed, whatever the evidence'.

It is dangerous to generalize carelessly on this subject. To say that all policemen were, by inclination, colour-prejudiced would be to ignore the efforts of many sincere officers who have worked hard for better understanding, men who are genuinely concerned about the situation and worried about the future. To deny categorically that many police are prejudiced, on the other hand, would be ridiculous. The ordinary policeman shares the general opinion of so many working-class white citizens about coloured immigrants. He believes that a man who chooses to leave his own country to seek a better life in Britain should accept the prevailing standards of conduct. 'They know their rights all right,' said a Birmingham sergeant. 'They know all about complaints against the police, I can tell you. Soon as you speak to one he's on at you, "Don't you touch me, copper, what's your number, man?" I'll tell you this, I've never backed down to a white man when I've been in this uniform, and I'm not backing down to a black.'

This determination not to lose face is shared by both sides in police-immigrant confrontations. In areas with high immigrant population, many policemen believe that they are forced to act strictly in law enforcement because any relaxation will be taken as a sign of weakness. The immigrants see every police action against them in terms of colour, making complaints inevitable. 'They complain out of force of habit,' said a London detective. 'Search them and find anything, they'll say you planted it. Take a voluntary statement, they'll say you beat them up. Call one as a prosecution witness against another one, he'll swear on oath that you threatened him if he wouldn't give evidence. They'll lie from morning till night, and they know it's lies.'

A frequently mentioned remedy for the current situation is the recruitment of many more coloured policemen. The official line is that coloured candidates will be recruited if they are of the same standard as white applicants. Police recruiting authorities insist that they get very few applications from coloured men and that most of these have to be rejected because of the low calibre of the applicants. It is true that coloured people rarely apply to join the force. This may in itself be indicative of the low opinion which immigrants have of the police. Just as in Northern Ireland the Royal Ulster Constabulary has never managed to recruit more than about ten per cent of its members from the Catholics, so young coloured men seem to regard joining the police as a form of betrayal of their own kind. The much-publicized 'Mansize 70' recruiting campaign of the Metropolitan Police produced only two applications from coloured men in the whole of 'B' division, which includes Notting Hill and Paddington.

'Immigrants are underprivileged in all employment fields,' said a West Indian who is influential in immigrant affairs, 'they have to overcome prejudice in every job except the lowest-paid ones. So, if a black man is good enough to join the police, he's good enough for a better job. The police only get fairly low calibre recruits from whites, so why should good quality blacks want the job?'

'Ten years ago,' said a recruiting officer, 'they wouldn't have been accepted. Now we'd be only too pleased to have them, if only to get people off our backs.'

Policemen are not enthusiastic about the prospect of large numbers of coloured recruits and see no reason why the force should go out of its way to recruit men simply because they are coloured, but the hostility which would have greeted black newcomers a few years ago (and which many chief officers feared would result from such recruitment today) has not materialized. It is a case of accepting the inevitable. Once it became clear that the unofficial colour bar (which undoubtedly operated until a few years ago) would have to be discarded, the way has been open for immigrants to join. Indeed, the first coloured recruit to the Metropolitan, a young man from the Leeward Islands, soon earned the reputation of being a good policeman and a good companion. At the height of the Notting Hill troubles he wrote on his own initiative to the *Police Review* to condemn black militants for their attacks on the police.

'What I would call the anglicized black man, or the Kenya Asian with a good education, would have no difficulty in the police,' said a Midlands inspector, 'but he would have to find acceptance in the same way as any new recruit has to. He's going to be judged on his ability. With most West Indians, I find it very hard to understand what they are saying, their speech is so indistinct. That's the kind of man who would find problems in the force, because every time he opened his mouth he'd simply be drawing attention to the fact that he was different from the others.'

The police believe that some elements among the immigrant communities encourage the idea that joining the force is joining the enemy. 'We've got our Black Power element in London,' said a Notting Hill inspector. 'They are stirring it up with the coloured youth. We are the enemy, the pigs, and we are supposed to go around beating them up. How do you expect to get coloured people to join the job if their own people call them Uncle Toms and won't have anything to do with them?'

Public reaction to coloured policemen is still an unknown factor. There have been too few black recruits to draw conclusions. 'You could put coloured constables on the beat in Hampstead Garden Suburb and you'd have no trouble,' said a London sergeant, 'the liberals would be falling over themselves to have them in for a cup of tea. Put one outside an Irish pub in Camden Town at closing time and see what happens.'

The police are firmly opposed to the recruitment of coloured police as part of a deliberate policy to provide West Indian or Asian officers to work in predominantly immigrant areas. 'You don't appoint policemen because they can get on with one part of the public,' said a Bradford officer, 'they've got to be acceptable to everyone.'

Against this, a London sergeant who has specialized in race relations said, 'We must have Asian policemen in the force just to deal with Asians. I do not believe that a white man can get inside the mind of a Sikh or a Pakistani. They have got to see their own people occupying positions of trust in the police force. Then they'll start to trust us. I'm convinced of this.'

This officer referred to the wall of silence which police so often encounter when making enquiries among Asians. One problem is that the rigid social codes they practise often clash with British criminal law. The tendency to take action against offenders within the community according to national custom has presented police with some baffling problems. Nor have they been able to overcome widespread distrust of the police by Asians who fear that unscrupulous officers will blackmail them. 'I got wind that someone was putting the black on illegal immigrants,' said a London detective. 'You know, thousands of Indians in Southall and Ealing have come here illegally. The whisper was that some detectives were demanding big money to keep quiet. No one would talk and no one would complain. I honestly don't believe there was a word of truth in it, but an Indian businessman who I respect assured me it was a fact. He said that some immigrants kept coming to him for advice, asking if they should pay. He says he told them not to pay, but to go to the police station and complain. The trouble was, they shouldn't have been here and they were frightened of being deported. So, he says, they paid. I think that what was happening was that some cunning bastard among them knew they were here illegally and was getting money out of them by pretending it was for the police. But how do you find out when no one will tell you anything?'

Many high-ranking policemen take a close interest in what happens in America. John Mckay, the Chief Inspector of Constabulary, said in an address to police authorities in 1970 that some people believed that America's present was Britain's future and said that if this was true, the outlook in Britain was a gloomy one. The 1970 picture in America was of black policemen becoming increasingly militant in their demands for equal treatment, with widespread allegations of discrimination within police departments. Associations of black policemen were critical of departmental policies towards coloured people and there had even been gun battles between white and black police. Significantly, the strongest supporters of George Wallace in the 1968 presidential elections were white policemen. If a poll were conducted among British policemen, I feel confident that Enoch Powell would emerge as the most popular politician in the country. 'Powell is the only politician who tells the truth,' is a statement I have heard often enough from many policemen.

So far, none of the handful of coloured policemen in Britain has been promoted. 'If I had to take orders from a black sergeant, I'd take them,' said a young London constable. 'It wouldn't make any difference to me.' An older policeman said, 'Provided he'd been promoted on merit, it wouldn't matter about his colour. Just so long as he wasn't pushing his weight about.'

Main areas of conflict between police and immigrants are those which arise from environmental problems: housing disputes between landlord and tenant; illicit drinking parties; different social codes; and, in particular, a lack of understanding of police powers in Britain.

'We've had it drummed into us at the training school that we don't interfere between man and wife or take sides in domestic disputes which are not police matters,' said a young constable in Notting Hill. 'If a black calls the police in, he takes it for granted that we'll take his part, because he's sent for us. If we don't do anything, then we're against him because he's black. All we can do is tell him to go and see the Citizens' Advice Bureau or a solicitor. He wants us to lock someone up for him, or get his money back by force.'

Contrary to widespread belief, immigrants do not in themselves present the police with abnormal crime problems. 'If you take them as a whole,' said a senior officer in the Black Country, 'they are probably more law-abiding than white people. The Asians certainly are. They deal with a lot of their own black sheep and we never get to hear about it. Their social codes are very strict.' 'You can't lump them all together,' said another Midlands officer, 'We've got all sorts here. Some of the Jamaicans are right villains, but some are the nicest people going. There's a church on my patch that used to be a Methodist chapel. Then it was a warehouse. Now some Jamaicans have it and it's packed every Sunday. You can hear them singing half a mile down the road. They go to church in their Sunday best and the kids are a picture. We don't have any trouble, in fact it's just the opposite. If any of their kids get into trouble, there's hell to pay when father gets home.'

The police regard the racial implications in the arrest of a coloured man for a crime as incidental. 'A criminal's a criminal, no matter what his colour is,' is a frequent police comment. Policemen will detest a West Indian who lives on a prostitute's earnings because they have always loathed this type of offender, not because he is black. Dislike in this case might be heightened by the racial overtones, but police action is dictated by the offence, not the offender.

'We could avoid half the trouble between police and immigrants if we compromised,' said a Midlands inspector. 'It would be easy enough to turn a blind eye to cannabis, for instance. But that's just buying a bit of time. If we started to go easy just for the sake of a quiet life with the blacks, two things would happen. The whites would start screaming about prejudice against them, and the blacks would take advantage.'

The police know that many immigrants are puzzled by the vastly different role of the police here from that of the police in their homeland. 'Indians are frightened to death of the police,' said a London officer who has studied police-public relations in India recently, 'and when you see how brutal and corrupt the Indian police are, you begin to understand why. It will take Indians in Britain years to overcome their fear of all policemen.'

In Notting Hill, the police have been criticized for insensitivity and harassment. It is alleged that they have raided a local youth club used exclusively by coloured youths, on the slightest pretext. The police answer would be that the police have always acted on information or reasonable suspicion. This inflexibility is typified by the police attitude towards the more gregarious features of West Indian social life. 'They are always complaining that we break up innocent house parties,' said a Notting Hill inspector. 'They are not ordinary parties as we know them. There was a lot in the papers when we were supposed to have raided a kid's birthday party. What wasn't said was that it was two in the morning and they were selling drinks and raising Cain in the street.'

The refusal of the police to apply different standards in their dealings with immigrants not only makes tension inevitable, it is regarded by some close observers as a form of discrimination in reverse. 'We get sociologists saying that there must be a different approach by the police because of the different customs of immigrant communities,' said a Midlands senior officer. 'What they mean, I suppose, is that if cannabis is all right in their own countries, we shouldn't interfere, rather like opium smoking used to be tolerated in the East End. But have the police the right to impose two standards of policing in an area, one for immigrants and one for whites? I'm all for increased understanding, but it has to begin with the immigrant, not with the policeman.'

The police have made some contribution towards better understanding. Local training schemes now include some (but still very little) training on immigrant matters, and nearly every area with a sizeable proportion of immigrants has its police community liaison officer. These officers find that suspicion of their activities is not confined to immigrants. 'I've found it easier to be accepted by black leaders than some policemen,' said a London chief inspector engaged on community relations. 'The older ones think it's just a gimmick and that I can't do anything positive. In some cases, I'm even accused of undermining police authority because I've listened to complaints and tried to sort them out.'

Immigration problems contain potential dangers to long-established bonds of understanding between local police and the white residents of areas with high immigration. White people expect that a policeman will automatically be on their side in a dispute with a coloured man. 'People round here don't like the Race Relations Act and things like community relations committees,' said a police liaison officer. 'I've had white people asking me why I've got so much time to spare to help blacks when there's supposed to be a shortage of police. We knocked off a gang of white youths for beating up black kids and some of them were sent to detention centres. After that, policeman got the cold shoulder down that way for a long time. It wasn't a question of right or wrong, people just thought that if the blacks hadn't come there wouldn't have been any trouble in the first place.'

Integration, the dream of an end to racial problems by the gradual assimilation of all immigrants into a multi-racial Britain, is not regarded as a practical possibility by many policemen. 'We have to spend a lot of time sorting out arguments between coloureds, not just white and coloured,' said a Brixton officer, "You lose track of who hates who, but if you want an example of real prejudice you'll find it in the way a West Indian from a big island treats one from a small island. They aren't even integrated with themselves.'

The complaints of police assaults on prisoners are so commonplace that some policemen adopt a resigned attitude about them. 'As soon as you have a coloured bloke in the cells,' said a station officer in London, 'you just sit back and wait for the Black Power to come in with a lawyer and a doctor. The lawyer wants bail and the doctor wants to examine him to count the bruises.'

Police resentment of Black Power's extravagant abuse is prompted by a genuine belief that the majority of immigrants, if not favourably disposed to police, are not against them. 'Most immigrants in this area,' said a Smethwick policeman, 'just want to be left alone. It's only a few who look for trouble. If other people, mostly outsiders, will stop stirring things up we'll manage.'

The 'stirring-up' comes from both sides. Each outburst from black militants is countered by demonstrations from extreme right-wing groups. 'We've had fascist newsheets circulating here,' said a police community relations officer in London. 'In their own way, they are as bad as the rubbish which Black Power puts around. What I object to is that the 'Keep Britain White' lot take it for granted that we are on their side. Some of them were in gaol under 18B during the war.'

The ordinary policeman is not interested in the wider social implications of the immigration question . He is fully occupied with the problems as it affects him in his work. All the same, one finds little optimism about the future. 'It can only get worse,' said the sergeant in Leeds. 'They are getting better-organized and as they do the white people will get nasty. We've had Paki-bashing in Leeds and it died down quickly, but the problem's getting bigger all the time. The real trouble will start when the coloureds have enough teenagers to pick a fight with the whites. They aren't like their parents. They won't stay in the house with the door locked when the trouble starts.'

'What I can't understand,' said a Northampton constable, 'is why they don't go home if they don't like it here. No one asked them to come.'

11 Demonstrations

The senior officer of the Royal Ulster Constabulary, standing beside me in the rainswept square in Londonderry on a bitingly cold January afternoon, thought I was trying to make a point at the expense of his force. 'Oh yes, they don't have any trouble in London, I'll give you that,' he said. 'Do you know why? Because they can flood any area with a sea of blue, that's why. Three nights ago I had thirty men to deal with a mob trying to break into that Guildhall, and we were keeping another thousand inside wanting to get out and have a go at the others, every man with a chair leg. We're just the meat in the sandwich here. I'd like to see the Metropolitan if they had to watch their backs and their fronts at the same time, as we have.'

It was the beginning of 1969, before Ulster rioting became a routine ingredient of television news, when viewers were still horrified at the blazing buildings, the petrol bombs, the baton-swinging police and the water cannons amid the bricks and paving stones. It all seemed so foreign, so akin to the previous year's rioting in Berlin and Paris. In London, the Metropolitan Police had touched the high point of public approval a few weeks earlier when the great October Demonstration, which the press had expected to mark the beginning of Chicago-style rioting in London, had turned out to be a pleasant stroll in the autumn sunshine. What had the violence and hatred of Northern Ireland to do with Britain?

It was a question I kept thinking about as I went round Londonderry, talking to policemen who had just been in the thick of the fighting and whose faces bore the scars. There was the young sergeant from a small station on a hill above Derry, who showed me the charred wall beneath a bedroom window. If the petrol bomb had been a few inches higher it would have landed on his baby's cot. There was the constable who had lived and worked among the people of the Bogside for years: 'I thought I knew these people. I liked it here. Honestly I did. Now I just want to get right away from Derry.' There were the men of the RUC's Reserve Force, known as the Riot Squad, and hated by the majority of Catholics, resting in the naval barracks and looking like battle-weary troops after days in the front line. They were complaining about the incompetence of senior policemen who stayed safe in Belfast and issued conflicting orders over the telephone.

The accusations surrounding the now legendary students' march were still front-page news as I spoke to the Reserve Force men who had accompanied the peace march when it was ambushed by militant Protestants at Burntollet. A sergeant (then known as a 'head constable') told me of the police bus which was ambushed at dead of night as it was taking injured policemen back to Belfast after the Burntollet incident: 'They were waiting at a bridge, God knows how many. There wasn't a man in the back who could have lifted a little finger. I just yelled at the driver to keep going and if any fucker got in the way, he could run the bastard over.'

A few days later, at Newry, the police high command decided on a sudden change of tactics. The ranks of police faced the civil rights demonstrators from behind their barriers, with police buses between them. A few hotheads in the crowd, denied direct physical contact with the police, attacked the buses and set them on fire, as the police intended that they should. It was to prove the government's point that the civil rights demonstrators were basically violent.

While the authorities at Stormont and RUC headquarters were congratulating themselves on their propaganda victory at Newry, the RUC men who had been ordered to stand and watch their tenders burn were puzzled and angry. They were veterans of years of skirmishes with Catholic and Protestant mobs. 'They shouldn't have let them burn the tenders,' said one man, 'and they shouldn't have made us hold back. In the old days, we'd have gone in and cracked heads for them. Now they're frightened of a television camera.'

I mention the troubles of the RUC because it is important to remember that, even in a part of the United Kingdom, it is by no means traditional for the police to play an impartial and tolerant role in political or social unrest. To the Catholics in Ulster, the police are and always have been the symbol of Unionist authority. Because of the political situation in the province, for fifty years the police had a dual responsibility in which the peace-keeping role was always subordinated in times of crisis to that of maintaining internal security against what the government regarded as invaders from the south.

One result of the continuing violence in Ulster has been the virtual neutralization of the police. Following the Hunt Report in 1970, an attempt was made to 'anglicize' the RUC by ending its paramilitary function and disarming its members, leaving security problems to the army. In effect, the result has been to exclude effective policing from the worst trouble spots, the notorious 'no-go' areas, and to create a situation in which the army has assumed both roles. The police themselves initially supported the major reforms introduced by Hunt. They wanted to assume a role in Ulster society similar to the police in the remainder of the United Kingdom, but a series of murders of unarmed policemen and diminishing public confidence in the political leadership has brought some disillusionment.

Ulster must be regarded as an object lesson for those who allow their impatience with occasional outbursts of civil disorder in Britain to lead them to demand 'tougher' police action. The RUC has tried such methods for half a century, with disastrous results. Yet the RUC man is justified in rejecting easy comparisons with other British police forces. He has always been occupied in keeping two violent factions apart, as distinct from recent police experience with demonstrations in London, where the police have dealt with one large gathering bent on a common object.

What happened in London in October 1968 was hailed around the world as a triumph of British moderation and the tolerance of the good-humoured bobby. But it was more than that; it was the culmination of years of experience of dealing with flashpoint situations, from the labour riots of the nineteenth century, the pitched battles between fascists and communists between the wars, and the era of 'punch-up' politics which have been a feature of London weekends throughout the sixties.

It has not always been a story of impeccable police work. There was the famous Trafalgar Square fiasco in 1962 when CND was at its height. The Metropolitan Commissioner had banned a projected march down Whitehall. The huge crowd sat in the square, waiting for midnight when the commissioner's order would expire. A senior officer gave the order for the square to be cleared, leading to violence. More recently, the police had made tactical mistakes in the use of police horses and in confining large numbers of demonstrators in small spaces, with consequent attacks on police cordons. It was significant, however, that throughout this period senior officers at Scotland Yard had been studying the lessons learned in successive major demonstrations and, as a result, the policy of generous co-operation which succeeded so brilliantly in October 1968 was devised.

The police were probably as surprised as the general public that the event turned out to be such a peaceful affair (apart from the action of a Maoist fringe, which broke away from the agreed route to try to storm the US Embassy). They had been affected by the massive publicity build-up and the atmosphere of near-hysteria which preceded it. 'We were given a much longer briefing than usual,' said a West End constable who could not remember precisely how many times he had performed weekend duty at demonstrations. 'The chief inspector kept on about the whole world watching us and how we had to keep calm and not be provoked.'

'We waited in the Strand for hours,' said another constable. 'There were crowds lined up on the pavements and I
thought they were like a coronation crowd, waiting to see the
procession. I was in front of Rhodesia House, where we really
thought there would be trouble. You could hear them a mile
off, chanting "Ho, Ho, Ho Chi-minh" and it was a bit
nerve-wracking. Then when we first saw them, all linked arms
and right across the road, with all the banners and red flags, it
was worse. But we'd heard that there'd been no trouble in
Fleet Street and it was a help to see our lads strolling along
chatting to them.'

'That's what did it,' said a student leader afterwards, 'all
the police smiling and chatting. You can't get annoyed with a
chap you've been talking to for hours, can you?'

In retrospect, it is easy to dismiss the scare stories which
preceded the October march, but the tension at the time was
real. If at any stage along the march the police had attempted
to interfere with its progress, the result could have been
different. 'I remember getting home very late that night,' said
another constable. 'My wife was sitting in front of the fire.
The telly wasn't on. She was just sitting there, staring. She
just asked me if I wanted anything to eat. She didn't mention
the demo, but I knew what she'd been through.'

It was during the fracas at the US Embassy that a
photographer snapped a demonstrator's boot at the moment
of impact with a policeman's head. The picture seemed to
sum up all the futility and viciousness of violence directed at
the unarmed British policeman, and brought home the
dangers faced by the police on these occasions. Other than
this, the October demonstration had been remarkable for its
lack of incident, so much so that a senior Scotland Yard
official was quoted as saying that the whole thing was 'a
damp squib', a remark which brought an angry reaction from
at least one policeman: 'What the hell did he want, a battle?'

In the years that have followed the October demonstration
London has seen nothing remotely comparable with it in size,
unless one includes the TUC-organized rally against the

ndustrial Relations Bill. Instead, the police in the capital and elsewhere have been kept busy with more spontaneous affairs, ranging from protests against white South African rugby tourists to miscellaneous demonstrations against foreign embassies, mostly by their own nationals. 'The worst kind of demonstration is the one you're not ready for,' said a policeman at West End Central. 'We just get a few hours notice, sometimes not even that. Some of these people are real headcases. They want a fight to get on television, and it's amazing how the TV people get to know in advance that something's going on.'

The policeman on demonstration duty expects trouble. He knows that violence is likely and that his own actions on the day can land him in all kinds of difficulties. 'There was this little chap with glasses in Grosvenor Square,' said a constable, 'he was more or less hiding behind a hedge. I'd watched him for a bit and noticed how he kept running up to anywhere where there seemed to be something happening, then coming back to this same spot. I thought at first that he was a reporter, so I didn't bother him. But then we had to take a banner from some lunatic who was using it as a lance and we broke it in half. Next thing I know there's this little bloke snapping a flashbulb at me. My mate grabbed hold of him and told him to F off. He's got an armband on and says, "I'm an official observer from the National Council for Civil Liberties. I want your name and number, I'm reporting you." Next thing he's straight through the hedge, camera and the lot. Just a push, mind. Lucky he wasn't locked up for obstruction.' That incident figured in a lengthy dossier submitted to the Home Secretary by the NCCL.

Many policemen accuse the press of provoking trouble at demonstrations, and this applies especially to television. 'We had this crowd hemmed in in North Audley Street,' said an inspector, referring to the Maoist group at the October 1968 demonstration. 'They were quiet enough until someone switched on a television light and shouted "Charge." And they did just that, just for the cameras. If I get close to a television camera in future, I'll smash it. They cause half the trouble.' Television concentrates on the sporadic violent episode to secure graphic pictures. Viewers are shown disturbing shots of police manhandling demonstrators, sometimes giving a wholly distorted impression of the whole event. Often, the same scenes are used over and over again, usually to illustrate some point in a documentary about the police.

The police see no reason to differentiate between a criminal assault committed by a drunken hooligan and one by a political demonstrator. In fact, they are more resentful of student violence, feeling that people with the intelligence to reach a university have no excuse for breaking the law. 'I'd have given my right arm to go to university,' said an inspector, 'but when I was their age there were some real fascists to deal with. These kids have everything on a plate and our taxes keep them there, to study, not to cause trouble.'

Officially, the police attitude to demonstrations is fairly non-committal. They are looked on as a nuisance, and policemen who have lost their chance of weekend leave cannot be expected to be sympathetic to the cause involved. The Home Secretary of the day came under strong pressure to ban the October 1968 demonstration because of the fear of extreme violence. Acting on police advice, he took a calculated risk in allowing it to go on. The result was that Mr Callaghan was able to say afterwards that the event had been a triumph for democracy: 'In no other country in the world could this have happened today.' If, on the other hand, things had gone wrong there would have been a major political row over the Home Secretary's 'blunder'. What was not mentioned was that, in their efforts to avoid confrontation, the police bent the law in permitting the march to occupy the whole of the streets it covered.

When demonstrators are arrested for assaulting the police, the force gets indignant when magistrates show leniency. 'One or two London stipendiaries won't have any nonsense,' said a London inspector. 'They either send them down or remand them in custody if they plead not guilty. It doesn't do the hard cases any good but the others will never bother you again. Once they've been inside a prison, all the glamour wears off.' Most policemen would have endorsed the angry reaction of Mr William Palfrey, chief constable of Lancashire, when magistrates imposed nominal fines on demonstrators who had been arrested at a Springbok match. 'Find them not guilty if you want to,' said Mr Palfrey, 'but don't fine them three pounds!'

In 1970, there were more than five hundred demonstrations in London, most of them small affairs. Experience has given the Metropolitan Police an expertise that provincial forces cannot match. This has meant that when demonstrations occur outside London, local police are aften accused of over-reacting. It was noticeable that the strongest complaints about the Springbok tour concerned the match at Swansea. 'Demands for full independent investigations after the event are futile,' said a London inspector. 'If people go on a demonstration and start breaking the law, they're going to get hurt'.

The police are well aware of the dangers of the so-called urban guerilla tactics which might come to replace mainly peaceful demonstrations in this country, and the spate of 'bombing' incidents which began in London in 1970 might have been the first signs that Britain was in for something like the epidemic of bombings which has replaced mass protest in the United States. Many policemen would say that this is the inevitable result of making concessions to persistent protest. The apparent unwillingness of university authorities to deal firmly with student unrest is regarded as an example. The majority of the force opposed the decision to cancel the 1970 cricket tour by the white South Africans. 'It's a disgusting thing when a Home Secretary gives in to hooligans,' said a London inspector. 'If the law says its legal to play cricket, anyone who tries to stop them is breaking the law.'

No one who has seen anything of what happens in

demonstrations in other countries would challenge the British policeman's claim to pre-eminence in the art of tolerant control. The police must acknowledge that their success owes much to the reasonable conduct of most of the people who take part in protest, for traditional methods of dealing with demonstrations can be persevered with only so long as there is a corresponding absence of violence towards the police. The danger of an expansion of violent protest is that the police themselves will be forced to react in like manner. If that happens, peaceful strolls through London will belong to history.

12 The women in the force

The enactment of the Equal Pay Bill in 1970 had special significance for Britain's four thousand policewomen, for it contained a clause forbidding discrimination between men and women police officers in pay and hours of duty. 'If it hadn't been for Barbara Castle,' said one woman inspector at this time, 'we'd have stayed on ninety per cent of the men's scales for ever. We never had the guts to stand up and shout for it.' For years, women members of the Police Federation were lukewarm to the subject. Some, who enjoyed the concessions of shorter hours and extended meal breaks, opposed equal pay because it meant the end of such perks. Only the small minority of dedicated career policewomen resented the lower pay scales. 'If there had been a referendum amoung the policewomen on the subject,' said a woman superintendent, 'they would have voted against it.'

If official details of length of service in the police is a reliable guide, only about one policewoman in ten makes the force a career. Over half the women constables are under twenty-five and only about one third stay for more than five years. Marriage is the main reason for high wastage. Although the force no longer requires women to resign on marriage, most find that the obligation to work shifts conflicts with their role as housewives, particularly when they have married outside the force. For some years, the Home Office has encouraged the introduction of a scheme to permit married women to return to the force as part-timers, but many policewomen regard this as a retrograde step which would damage their own career expectations and the scheme has been delayed by haggling over pension plans. 'The part-timer would be able to pick and choose her hours,' said one policewoman, 'and we'd have to fill in with the awkward shifts.'

The high wastage rate has hindered the ambitions of those senior women officers who have aimed for full professional equality. If the great majority of women regard the job in such temporary fashion, there is no real incentive for police authorities to improve women's job opportunities and their career structure. It has taken policewomen just over fifty years to reach their present standing in the service and even now they receive little more than grudging recognition from many of their male colleagues. 'Very few men look upon us as equals,' said a woman senior officer. Between the wars, just about the only issue which united the autocratic chief officers with the Federation was a common dislike of policewomen. They first emerged in the First World War. A group of well-meaning social workers took it upon themselves to patrol London's West End to offer unwanted help and advice to prostitutes. A formidable eccentric, Mrs Damer-Dawson, was their leader and she dressed her helpers in police-style uniforms. They were a considerable embarrassment to the police, who had to keep an eye on them as they patrolled. An official group of voluntary patrols was formed in London to concentrate on moral welfare among women in munitions factories and the hordes of camp-followers around the garrisons. Friction between the two was considerable and at times hilarious. Eventually, the voluntary patrols were recognised in preference to Mrs Damer-Dawson's middle-class do-gooders, and formed the nucleus of the first group of policewomen in 1919.

Attempts were made to kill the infant service almost as soon as it was started. The authorities used the excuse of national economics to disband the force in the early twenties and had it not been for a fierce campaign by Lady Astor, they would have disappeared altogether. She secured a concession by which a small force was retained during the depression years.

Policewomen were involved in the major scandal that led to the Royal Commission on Police Powers and Procedure in 1929. A wealthy man with connections in high places, Sir Leo Money, was arrested in Hyde Park with a young woman. The charge against him was dismissed and questions were asked in Parliament. During the furore, the girl in the case (who had a good reputation) was taken to Scotland Yard and interrogated by detectives. A woman inspector was present but was ordered from the room when the questioning began. The outcome of the Royal Commission report was a firm recommendation that policewomen should be employed in order to deal with these 'delicate' matters — a recommendation made in the teeth of police opposition.

Opposition to or resentment of policewomen in the force has been motivated by the policeman's professional pride and his strong belief that police work is man's work. Even today, attempts to place women in specialist departments such as CID and the traffic branch will produce strong reactions from men. 'Very few women can do the job properly,' insisted a Yorkshire inspector. 'They don't do nights and they certainly can't do the jobs a man does. If I put a woman outside the Miners' Welfare on Saturday night, I'd be for the high jump on Monday morning.' To this most women would retort that many policemen do not perform shift duties. 'The truth is,' said a woman with over twenty years' service, 'that the idea of equality hurts their egos.'

A woman inspector in the Metropolitan CID said; 'I could think of many men who haven't done half as much real police work as I have. Believe me, when it comes to crime the female of the species can be a hundred times worse than a man.' Confirmation of this view comes from the fact that the Criminal Injuries Compensation Board dealt with eighteen claims in 1970 from policewomen who suffered relatively severe injuries after being assaulted on duty.

It takes a woman with courage and common sense to handle some of the screaming, hysterical and half-demented female prisoners who sometimes create havoc in a police station. 'The first time it happened to me was straight out of training school,' said a woman constable in London. 'The sergeant came in a panic and said, "Cells, quick." She was a middle-aged hag, fighting drunk on VP wine and her language was vile. She'd clawed the face of a young constable and she was stripping off and swearing blue murder that the sergeant had tried to rape her. It's funny looking back, but I was dead scared at the time. I just went right in and smacked her face, hard. It was all I could think of, but it worked. It always does.' A policewoman can achieve a degree of equal status among policemen by proving herself to be their equal in professional competence, but only a small minority find acceptance on these grounds.

'The economics of having women in the force are crazy,' said a superintendent. 'It costs just as much to train them as men. With a male recruit you are taking a big chance. He may stay thirty years or go in a year, but with women you know it's almost certain that she'll be out in a few years. All training and experience wasted. We need some women, but they should be specialists and we would stop pretending that they're all-rounders. If we restricted their duties to essential women's work, dealing with women and kids, we could cut the numbers in half.' This was the role envisaged from the start for policewomen. It has been the constant pressure of a few women at the top (and senior posts for women are scarce) that has forced open closed doors. Policemen look on the posting of women to specialist departments as a lessening of their own career opportunities.

The separation of policewomen from the main body is emphasized by their own career structure. Although women are subject to the overall control of chief officers and must obey instructions from supervisory officers, their promotion is dictated by their numbers in each force, and women with rank can, in practice, only give orders to other women. Some years ago, a women inspector in Scotland applied for a vacant chief constableship in a small force. Her application was treated as a joke. In the current climate, Britain will have a woman Prime Minister long before the first woman chief constable is appointed.

Policewomen have their own disciplinary problems. Because the majority of women in the force are not careerists, those who are promoted tend to have little in common with young women constables. In 1971 it was revealed that serious allegations had been made against a senior woman officer in Scotland in respect of her alleged treatment of junior policewomen and a Member of Parliament demanded an inquiry. Whatever the true facts in this case, it is certainly not uncommon for younger women to find the discipline imposed by their own officers irksome. 'Give me a man in charge any day,' said a woman constable in London. 'Some of the women we have treat you like dirt. If they take a dislike to you, they can make your life a misery. I've known girls pack up in tears just because of the bitchiness of one woman inspector.' Women supervisory officers, on the other hand, do have disciplinary problems. They feel a direct responsibility for the younger women working in a wholly male environment and their sense of dedication to the job makes them resent irresponsibility in women officers. 'Men sergeants and inspectors are not much help to us,' said a woman inspector. 'They can laugh and joke with the girls and show off their masculine charms. We are the ones who have to keep them in order, and that's why we're the bitches.'

Until it is finally decided whether policewomen are to become wholly assimilated within the service, performing duty in every department on the same terms as men, or be restricted to the more socially oriented tasks of dealing with women and children, they will continue to lack a clearly defined role in the force.

Few would deny that in the latter field policewomen have been an unqualified success. One needs only to observe the work of policewomen in areas such as the West End, a mecca for girls who have absconded from institutions or simply wandered from home, to realize their importance to the service. Invariably, it is the policewoman who has to deal with the woman shoplifter, stunned by the shock of arrest in most cases, and provide a vital spark of humanity at this traumatic moment. 'You've got to draw a distinction between the hard case who makes a living off the stores and knows all the tricks and the little old woman who just yielded to temptation,' said a Yorkshire policewoman. 'Some of them just go to pieces when they're brought in. That's when we are needed.'

In cases of child neglect, policewomen are valuable in comforting the small victims and, on occasion, putting the fear of retribution into the parents. 'In many ways our girls are the best social workers you can find,' said a male superintendent. 'They haven't only learned their job in a training college and they don't have any illusions about human nature. They can talk to people in a much more down-to-earth way than, say, a probation officer, and because they have a uniform people take much more notice of them.'

The service is not blind to the good public-relations asset it possesses in its women members. The public in general seems to be better disposed towards policewomen, and there are probably fewer complaints pro rata than with the men. 'It can get a bit much, though,' said a woman sergeant, 'we're always being sent to give talks to Mother's Unions and Townswomen's Guilds.'

13 Conclusion

Tommy Butler was the senior Scotland yard detective who became famous for his dogged pursuit of the great train robbery fugitives. He trailed one of the gang who broke out of Birmingham prison to Canada, and went all over Europe in search of another. His tenacity earned him the press tag, the 'Grey Ghost', and when he was due to retire he was allowed to stay on to try to finish the job. When he died only a few months after retirement, few of his colleagues were unduly surprised. The idea of Tommy Butler being anything other than a working policeman had always been unthinkable. Butler was a quiet, colourless and humourless man who generated little warmth. He typified a small group of policemen who are dedicated in the most unambiguous sense of the word and often ruthless in their pursuit of ambition. He lived only for his work and when he died, colleagues who had worked closely with him could recall only his occasional visit to a cinema to see a Western (doubtless one in which the US marshal hunted outlaws) as evidence of some outside interest. Men such as Butler are widely respected in the police force because of their devotion to the job and their supreme competence as thief-catchers. Being a bachelor, Butler did not ask his family to share in his total involvement with his work, avoiding a situation which has been the cause of much unhappiness in the marriages of other detectives.

The 'hundred-per-cent coppers' see themselves apart from society almost deliberately. They accept that their roles as policemen extend over twenty-four hours a day, seven days a week. Over the years, they become so caught up in the continuous routine of police existence — the early morning start, the enquiries, court work, evenings in pubs with fellow detectives — that they seem to have no other life-style. One is made to wonder about the domestic situations they have left at home and the effect that the years have had on wives and children. The separation of such policemen from the community is largely self-imposed. Almost without exception the men who choose it are detectives, simply because all other branches of the service work a more or less standard shift system which does not impose the continual obligations of the CID.

The factors which set most other policemen apart from their fellow men are less obvious, and are often determined by the feelings of people outside the police. The ordinary citizen has an ambivalent approach to the police. He respects them for what he regards as their good points: their efficiency, their courtesy, occasionally their courage. He dislikes them for their apparent enjoyment of inconveniencing him, for instance when he is pulled up for a motoring offence, and for the guilty feeling he experiences when uniformed policemen appear in a pub a few minutes after closing time and he still has a drink in his hand.

Some separation of the police from the public is inevitable and even desirable. The policeman is expected to keep clear of anything overtly controversial, such as politics. It is unthinkable (as well as a criminal offence) for a policeman to go on strike for better pay and conditions. But any consideration of this matter of police 'apartness' must take account of the simple fact that 'the public' is not a homogeneous mass with a uniform attitude to the police. The individual policeman is no more set apart from every section of the public than he is able to be at one with everyone of his fellow citizens. Thus, articulate spokesmen of the radical students speak of the 'pig ethos', by which they mean the attitude of the policeman who has joined the job because he is in love with authority and revels in the interaction of the police stations, where he meets wholly like-minded authoritarians united in the detestation of all forms of protest and noncomformity. The young motorist with his high-powered sports car sees every policeman as a face beneath a peaked cap, anxious to catch him in a radar trap and take away his licence.

Such special-interest groups apart, it is probably a mistake to assume that 'the public', meaning the nation as a whole, has any hard-and-fast views about its police. Sometimes, when there is a great deal of agitation going on about some aspect of police behaviour, Members of Parliament and editorial writers get worked up about what they blithely assume to be the state of public opinion. 'The public will not be satisfied,' we are told, 'until there is a fully independent system of complaints investigation.' The public, if the truth be told, could hardly care less about the subject.

The police themselves are prone to mistake the noise created by the few for the general view of the public, and to complain that people expect too much of them and are too quick to complain when things go wrong. This, at least in part, is one of the reasons why the police tend to go immediately on to the defensive at the first breath of criticism. There is a too-ready assumption that 'the public' has turned against them and is looking for a scapegoat.

What is fairly general in all public attitudes to the police, however, is that clear distinction between 'them' and 'us' by which the citizen refuses to identify his interests and responsibilities with those of the policeman. Thus the citizen says; 'This is not my affair. It is a job for the police.' The point made in police efforts to improve relations with the public is that there does exist such a communion of interests, that the police are doing a job that rightly belongs to all citizens. With few exceptions, the citizens want no part of it. Public non-co-operation can be either deliberate or instinctive: a refusal to assist a policeman struggling to arrest a thief or a general failure on the part of motorists to take elementary precautions to prevent vehicle thefts.

Some of the separation of the police from the population has been caused by the way in which the police service has developed. The force takes pride in its sheer professionalism and, by implication, despises amateurs (Special Constables) and other inferior law-enforcement agencies, such as probation officers and social workers. This inborn belief in the superiority of the police in their own field, and in the essential mysteries of policing, is behind the somewhat Luddite approach which the police have adopted towards civilianization within police stations.

Some of the recent changes in police organization, such as the amalgamations of forces and the introduction of new working methods with greater use of motor cars, have been criticized as tending to reduce still further police links with the community. It is true that the larger police forces are less subject to local control and influence and, following the reorganization of local government in the next few years, the question of a police force organized in regions, or even a national force, will be worth considering. The increased efficiency (in terms of speedy response to emergencies) resulting from more police cars has been obtained at the cost of some loss of contact with the public as fewer policemen walk the streets, but simple economics dictated the eventual disappearance of most of the beat bobbies.

The police as a group could do a lot to break down some of the invisible barriers which are sometimes erected between them and the people. The most positive step in this direction would be a policy-decision to get rid of the police houses. With close on half the total force already living in their own homes, completely divorced from a police environment, everything possible should be done to encourage the occupants of the remaining police houses to follow suit. One of the problems is that police authorities, in their postwar building plans, built so many police houses together that a simple transfer of ownership would do little to remove their occupants from an artificial and sometimes stifling police environment.

I sometimes doubt if the police fully appreciate just how introverted they are. A casual observer, visiting a police canteen or finding himself in policemen's company, would be struck by the fact that they are inveterate shop-talkers. Police social clubs, particularly where they are attached to police stations, tend to encourage this inward-looking attitude. Even in sport, some chief officers encourage their young men to play cricket and football against other police teams only, on the grounds that sporting conflict can lead to incidents which could damage the reputation of the force. Such a body as the International Police Association, although founded with the excellent purpose of fostering international friendship between police officers, may owe much of its success to the fact that it enables policemen who feel secure in a wholly police environment to take their holidays abroad with other policemen!

At a time when the pressures on the police are mounting steadily, there is a real need for police commanders to pay attention to the impact of police work on the family lives of policemen. Although most provincial forces have succeeded in introducing a five-day week for their members, there are still some forces where shifts are so arranged that the very last consideration is the convenience of the men. The effect of inconvenient shift-arrangements on domestic life can be disastrous, yet a few chief constables are still prepared to alter satisfactory systems to suit their own administrative requirements. Everything that remains in the modern police service which can have the effect of reducing the ordinary policeman's opportunities to lead a normal life in the community should be carefully examined to see whether its retention can be justified. In particular this applies to the police service's antiquated notion of discipline.

Slowly, almost reluctantly, the police service has been coming round to the need to reconsider its traditional role in the community. For more than a century it has been deemed sufficient for the police to act purely as law enforcers, with the additional duty since the invention of the motor car of protecting life on the roads, Now it is beginning to be understood that this limited police function is not going to be enough in the future. More and more the police are finding themselves involved in situations where there is no ready-made remedy in the criminal law. It may be the growing drug problem, or simply all the environmental pressures of life in the inner city core, where human problems arise which may not involve any specific breach of law — landlord and tenant abuses, racial prejudice, and so on. These are still areas where the skilled social worker must be primarily involved, but no longer can the police show indifference to what, in the long term, will be the causes of real police problems. From this realization is emerging an understanding of the role of the ordinary policeman, not as another social worker, but as a social diagnostician, able to act within the community to bring to bear the social agencies which can deal with specialized problems. In a sense, this role was pioneered by the policewomen in the area of children in need of care, and now it can be extended to many other problems. As the chief constable of Birmingham said at the Police Federation seminar in 1971: 'A policeman must allow his social awareness to be a very positive part of his thinking when he is on duty, so that he can recognize the situations which might mean crime in the future, and either bring them to notice or highlight the need for action. He should begin to create a situation where it is natural, not unusual, for the police to show concern and interest in local affairs.'

But this concept is far removed from the idea of the policeman who is set apart from his fellow men. To be achieved to any significant degree, it requires a radical change of emphasis within the police service, away from the notion that a policeman is, first, last and always, a crime fighter. It would require a drastic change in the training programme of the force and, frankly, a change in the general pattern of police recruits. This done, more and more police resources (in other words, men and women) would have to be employed in areas where practical help is most needed. To be really effective, there would have to be a deliberate policy decision to concentrate the bulk of available manpower in such areas, even to a reduction in the amount of cover available in less difficult areas.

To the cynical observer of the police scene, this may sound like so much pious nonsense, because the belief that the police service is so hidebound in its own conservatism is perhaps more deeply rooted in some radical minds than the most fondly cherished police prejudices. In a few years' time if the recently revised Metropolitan recruit-training syllabus is given a fair opportunity and if the provincial training schemes are altered in the same way, the first real evidence of the ability and indeed the readiness of the police to change their traditional role may be seen.

John Alderson, the present Commandant of the Police College and formerly in charge of training in the Metropolitan Police, describes the principles underlying the revision of the Metropolitan training syllabus:

We stressed the present dilemma facing policemen from whom so much is asked by society, often unfairly. We started off by having regard to sensitivity and including in the early weeks of the training period elementary behavioural and social studies. We looked at society and took it to pieces. We dealt with policemen in London, the various neighbourhood differences, as between Tower Hamlets and Hampstead. We mentioned the social agencies available to the policeman in his daily work as a diagnostician, so that he could understand their role in society and activate them where necessary. We included in the programme concepts of aggression, prejudice and human relation to authority. Instead of teaching a policeman how to arrest a person, we taught him the social and humanitarian factors involved in this piece of police activity. This is a very large thing for young men of nineteen, with ordinary education, to grasp . . .

Indeed it is. It is also going to be a very hard thing for hard-bitten, down-to-earth working policemen of years of experience to grasp, still harder to persuade them that it is right that the police service should be ready to turn its back on the methods and basic approach which have served it so well for so long. Yet it must be done.

The police are also going to have to expand their own social involvement as part of, not instead of, their tasks of preventing and detecting crime. For, in the last analysis, this is still what a police force is for. That is why society sets aside a certain section of its citizens and calls them policemen, that is what society pays them to do. They will have to assume this additional burden, just as they have over the years shouldered other tasks, because they are the police, and society knows that its police will do whatever is asked of them, so long as it is humanly possible to do it.

In the years ahead the police will continue to be under-manned and overworked and, such being the order of things, usually they will be underpaid. Occasionally, some of them will be criticized and a few of them will go to gaol themselves. Frequently they will be attacked for doing their job in a way which someone thinks they should not have done it. Less frequently they will be congratulated for their devotion to duty, even their heroism.

There will be changes in the way they work. A policeman who retired ten years ago would not recognize the job as it is performed today. But whatever changes are made, it remains obvious that the British police will continue to enjoy their unique relationship with the public they serve. For all the difficulties, and for all the popular feeling that there is something indefinably 'different' about a policeman, it is not by accident that the traditional figure of the uniformed bobby is taken to epitomize all that is best in Britain and its way of life.

And that, after all, is nothing to be ashamed of.